LESSONS

FROM ONE

WORSHIP LEADER

TO ANOTHER

Raelynn Parkin

ISBN 13: 978-1-934379-10-3

Table of Contents

2

Dedication

This book is dedicated first of all
To my Lord who carried me through many stormy waters,
To my beautiful husband who loved me through it all,
And to my children who sacrificed their time with me
For the sake of the Call.
Also, for my Mom and Dad, my Mother and Father In-Law,
And all of my family who loved on me through hard times.
This book is also for those who have encouraged me,
Believed in me, and prayed for me.
You have all meant so much to me in my journey.

Preface

It is my sheer delight to share this book with you. I have lived and breathed many of these pages, and have come through many fires to impart these lessons to you. I once wondered why I was seeing so much going on in the church. The Lord let me know that this was just a little slice of what was going on in the entire Body of Christ. For some, these lessons may not necessarily reflect your experience or what you are going through. But some of you may find yourself in difficult times with little light at the end of the tunnel. If you are one of these, just keep reading as each chapter builds to the next chapter and pretty soon you may find yourself in a most glorious place. My heart is to let that one know that you are not alone, and there is victory on the other side of the heartache you may be experiencing. Hopefully there are strategies in these pages that can quickly help you to the other side as one reaching out their hand to help another brother or sister in need.

As each chapter unfolds for you, you may discover that this is really a journey from where the church currently is to where the Glory is, and those two shall meet. I am counting on it. I was at first concerned that there was too much scripture listed in these pages, as the Lord has really brought His Word alive to me in the area of worship. However, the Lord calmed my heart and let me know that there is Glory in His Word, and to leave it alone. There is Glory in Him, and He IS the Word. So in many places where I could have condensed the scriptural references, I left them completely in tact and in their context so that you could see the entire picture. You may be tempted to just skim over some of these passages, but I would encourage you to taste every Word. For there is much Glory in the scriptures that I believe the Lord wants you to partake, as he imparts many more revelations to you personally than I could capture in this book. The Lord may want to draw you into deeper waters, and I am merely offering you an introduction to step in.

I also referred to these truths as they first occurred in the scriptures, as they set the precedent for all other scriptures that follow. When studying law, you learn about the first precedent, the law that was first set that all other relevant cases refer to. I believe the same is true of the Word of God. God gives us so much meat in the first occurrence, there are principles that He applies to the rest of His Scripture, which may unlock the doors of the Glory that is later revealed. He may lead you to beautiful nuggets of your own as you delve into His Word. He is the Living, Breathing Word, and I don't think we will ever get the full revelation until we see Him face to face. We will be discovering how glorious He is for all eternity, and getting to know Him as He is.

When I lead worship, I am merely bringing you to the One who is everything you could possibly need. Hopefully you can enter into a personal worship experience as I open the door for you and introduce you to Him. My destination is forever going to be the Holy of Holies, and that is where I prayerfully lead the body. However, I don't believe it was ever my calling to just give the people a "fish," but to teach them "how to fish." My greater calling was to impart what the Lord has given me to the next generation of worshippers, and teach them how to also open those doors through worship, how to enter the Holy of Holies, how to carry the Glory, and how to lead the entire body of Christ into deeper waters of worship experience with him. This gives me great joy, to know that others can join me in this quest.

My ultimate prayer is that this is a transforming "Now" word for the Church, the body of Christ, and that it will transform worshippers, worship leaders, worship ministries, and all ministries of the Church. But most of all, my heart's desire is to see God's Glory return to the Church and the landscape of the Church to be transformed and renewed. It's a tall order, but I believe the precepts in this book tap into the Heart of the Father as he is seeking worshippers who will worship him in spirit and in truth. This book is the truth part, and may be a little strong in places, but the Spirit is in the actual demonstration of his Glory on the platform. Where it is strong, I pray that you receive this word in the spirit in which it was written, in love and intending to unite the body of Christ, and certainly not to offend anyone. Please feel free to share this book with your pastors as well as your worship ministers as I believe it will directly affect your worship in your church as well. But most of all I pray that it transforms the private worship of every believer who reads it. Whether you are musically inclined or not, these precepts are for the entire body of Christ, and for every area of ministry in the church.

So, let's begin this journey together and see where he takes us.

God's Blessings,

Raelynn Parkin

Chapter 1
Unless the Lord Builds the House

Unless the LORD builds the house, its build-
ers labor in vain. Unless the LORD watches
over the city, the watchmen stand guard in
vain.   - Psalms 127:1

This first chapter is just to set some ground
rules that should be observed in worship ministries both on and off the platform and by the
novice as well as the seasoned worship ministry
leaders. This is the House of the Lord. The
same house rules that apply to the whole house
apply here also.

The Holy Spirit must have two things in
order to feel welcome to come into agreement
with you, as manifested by His Anointing. His
Anointing just means "Yes, Yes, Yes," or "Yes,
that's me," or "Yes that is the perfect will of
God." Now the Holy Spirit can anoint on different levels, the good will of God, the acceptable or permissive will of God, or the perfect
will of God. We must allow the Holy Spirit

11

complete freedom to do whatever he wants, and realizing that he is holy, there must be certain conditions present so that he actually feels welcome and at home in his surroundings that he may come fully. I believe the only limitations of the Holy Spirit are when we limit him or his ability to enter in his fullness.

Divine Order

First things first: divine order. Throughout the Bible, God works only through divine order. He usually calls one to lead and then delegates authority to one that follows. The one who leads is the one who carries the vision of where the whole body is to go. This vision should line up with the pastor's vision. Each service will have a path to follow that the Holy Spirit wants to lead. The most "successful" service is the one where the Holy Spirit is allowed to fully lead worship, taking the entire body where he would have us go in order to accomplish everything he set out to do. It's in these times where the Holy Spirit is actually your true Worship Leader. This is what makes the worship leader's task so critical because it is their job to closely follow the Holy Spirit, to hear and see the direction he is going, and to lead the team and in turn the congregation in that direction.

Biblical Unity

Second: Biblical unity. Many things can have the appearance of unity and yet be in complete disarray. One type of false unity that is only surface deep, usually motivated by the flesh, is political unity. This is when you support someone in doing whatever their "thing" is so that in turn they will support you in yours. Some examples are: flattery, equality (everyone on equal footing; no clearly defined leader), political maneuvering, manipulation, the promotion of personal agendas, majority rule (in place of divine order), mutiny and rebellion. Gaining political power and favors in order to promote an idea, a direction, or an agenda is wrong. Following are some Biblical examples that we can glean from concerning divine order and biblical unity.

Remember, every time certain people rose up against Moses, God always backed his man. Numbers, chapter 12 depicts the story of when Aaron and Miriam, the brother and sister of Moses, opposed his leadership and authority by proposing the idea that they could prophesy equally as well as Moses could, in effect, they were equal to him and his standing with God. For this insolence, Miriam was struck with leprosy and left outside the camp for seven days. God will stand behind his authority, so it would be a good thing to find out where the spiritual authority is and stand with them, back them up, not go around their backs, and passing them up in the chain of authority.

Korah also led a rebellion against Moses. Korah and his group of Levites were given the privilege of ministering before the Lord, but they also were after the control of the priesthood which was delegated to Aaron and his sons. Korah and all his followers were supernaturally swallowed up by the earth to include their families and all their possessions with them. To see the entire scripture passage in its full context, read Numbers Chapter 16 as we will visit this passage later on. We will work with the following excerpt for now:

[1]<u>Korah</u> son of Izhar, the son of Kohath, the son of Levi, and certain Reubenites-Dathan and Abiram, sons of Eliab, and On son of Peleth—<u>became insolent</u> [2] <u>and rose up against Moses. With them were 250 Israelite men, well-known community leaders who had been appointed members of the council.</u> [3] <u>They came as a group to oppose Moses and Aaron and said to them, "You have gone too</u>

far! The whole community is holy, every one of them, and the LORD is with them. Why then do you set yourselves above the LORD's assembly?"

4 When Moses heard this, he fell facedown. 5 Then he said to Korah and all his followers: "In the morning the LORD will show who belongs to him and who is holy, and he will have that person come near him. The man he chooses he will cause to come near him. 6 You, Korah, and all your followers are to do this: Take censers 7 and tomorrow put fire and incense in them before the LORD. The man the LORD chooses will be the one who is holy. You Levites have gone too far!"

8 Moses also said to Korah, "Now listen, you Levites! 9 Isn't it enough for you that the God of Israel has separated you from the rest of the Israelite community and brought you near himself to do the work at the LORD's tabernacle and to stand before the community and minister to them? 10 He has brought you and all your fellow Levites near himself, but now you are trying to get the priesthood too. 11 It is against the LORD that you and all your followers have banded together. Who is Aaron that you should grumble against him?"

28 Then Moses said, "This is how you will know that the LORD has sent me to do all these things and that it was not my idea: 29

If these men die a natural death and experience only what usually happens to men, then the LORD has not sent me. ³⁰ But if the LORD brings about something totally new, and the earth opens its mouth and swallows them, with everything that belongs to them, and they go down alive into the grave, <u>then you will know that these men have treated the LORD with contempt."</u>

³¹ As soon as he finished saying all this, the ground under them split apart ³² and the earth opened its mouth and swallowed them, with their households and all Korah's men and all their possessions. ³³ They went down alive into the grave, with everything they owned; the earth closed over them, and they perished and were gone from the community. ³⁴ At their cries, all the Israelites around them fled, shouting, "The earth is going to swallow us too!" ³⁵ And fire came out from the LORD and consumed the 250 men who were offering the incense.

⁴⁷ So Aaron did as Moses said, and ran into the midst of the assembly. The plague had already started among the people, but Aaron offered the incense and made atonement for them. ⁴⁸ He stood between the living and the dead, and the plague stopped. ⁴⁹ <u>But 14,700 people died from the plague, in addition to those who had died because of Korah.</u>

50 Then Aaron returned to Moses at the entrance to the Tent of Meeting, for the plague had stopped.

- Numbers 16: 1-11, 28-35, 47-50

Even though the majority stood against Moses and Aaron, God stood with his man in authority who was righteous in his sight. Continued disagreement and grumbling against them resulted in even more being punished. I agree that the way God dealt with disobedience in the Old Testament was a little stronger than how he deals with believers of the cross. But God does operate by delegating authority to the ones he chooses, and eventually God deals with his own house first in order to maintain his righteous standards. Korah and his people were daily witnesses of the Lord's glory and yet they still rebelled against God's appointed leader. Therefore, since the Lord's glory and holiness are inseparable I believe this to be an example of why we are not currently seeing even an Old Testament measure of his glory let alone a New Testament level of demonstration. If his holiness is not an established work in our own lives which is then manifested on the platform, we won't stand up very well either. A New Testament example of this precept is the story of Ananias and Sapphira falling down dead when Peter exposed their deceit. In the early church, there was a level of Glory established in the presence of the Holy Spirit through Peter's leadership. We must prepare our hearts to come before Him in a consecrated manner, with clean hands and pure hearts. We will study this in more depth in a future chapter.

Take Up Thy Cross

Sometimes God will call one to lay down his/her life to pay the price for what the rest will get to enjoy merely through membership. When God calls one to be a leader over you, your job is to cover that leader in prayer, and to thank God that he didn't ask you to pay a heavy price for the level of anointing you get to partake of freely. You should also honor them, and realize that the lead duck, when flying in formation, cuts the wind (opposition) with their very face. So, you'd better have their back, because when they grow tired, you may have to slip into the lead position so they can rest. It will then be your face having to cut through the wind and the opposition. The greater responsibility before God is your leader, so honor them and serve them and the vision God has given them with everything you've got.

God is Your Promoter

God is your promoter, and if you have been faithful to serve another person's vision and help to plant their field, then when God looks upon you he will say you're ready for your own field. You can not supplant God's process of promotion. No personal serenades to your pastor and no buddying up with other members of leadership. God is showing your leaders who is spiritually mature and who is ready to lead. You cannot promote yourself. Promoting yourself by setting up your own leadership in place of your leader (outdoing them or showing them up) in no way ensures that God is going to entrust you with their mantle, anointing, place, or position.

Do you remember when Elisha asked Elijah for a double portion of his spirit, the mantle that Elijah operated in? God was not displeased with the request but gave Elisha one condition for him to receive his request; that if he saw Elijah go up to Heaven, then Elijah's mantle would be passed down to Elisha.

⁶And Elijah said unto him, Tarry, I pray thee, here; for the LORD hath sent me to Jordan. <u>And he said, As the LORD liveth,</u>

and as thy soul liveth, I will not leave thee. And they two went on.

⁷And fifty men of the sons of the prophets went, and stood to view afar off: and they two stood by Jordan.

⁸And Elijah took his mantle, and wrapped it together, and smote the waters, and they were divided hither and thither, so that they two went over on dry ground.

⁹And it came to pass, when they were gone over, that Elijah said unto Elisha, Ask what I shall do for thee, before I be taken away from thee. And Elisha said, I pray thee, let a double portion of thy spirit be upon me.

¹⁰And he said, Thou hast asked a hard thing: nevertheless, if thou see me when I am taken from thee, it shall be so unto thee; but if not, it shall not be so.

¹¹And it came to pass, as they still went on, and talked, that, behold, there appeared a chariot of fire, and horses of fire, and parted them both asunder; and Elijah went up by a whirlwind into heaven.

¹² And Elisha saw it, and he cried, My father, my father, the chariot of Israel, and the horsemen thereof. And he saw him no more: and he took hold of his own clothes, and rent them in two pieces.

¹³He took up also the mantle of Elijah that fell from him, and went back, and stood by the bank of Jordan;

¹⁴And he took the mantle of Elijah that fell from him, and smote the waters, and said, Where is the LORD God of Elijah? and when he also had smitten the waters, they parted hither and thither: and Elisha went over.

- 2 Kings 2:6-14 KJV

When God promoted Elijah (to Heaven) only then was the mantle free to pass to Elisha. Outside of God's timing, Elisha, who was much stronger and younger, could have attempted to snatch the mantle from Elijah at any time towards the end. This action would not have resulted in Elisha receiving his request but would have disqualified him from it.

Those Who Have Gone Before

The principle: "The son honored the father and in doing so, was granted the Godly desires of his heart." Elisha honored his spiritual father and waited for God's timing and in doing so received his inheritance freely which was the double portion of what Elijah had been given. Jesus, the Son, also honored the Father, and did nothing without first seeing what His Father did.

> [19] Jesus gave them this answer: "I tell you the truth, the Son can do nothing by himself; he can do only what he sees his Father doing, because whatever the Father does the Son also does.   - John 5:19

The fourth commandment applies here as well.

> [12] "Honor your father and your mother, so that you may live long in the land the LORD your God is giving you.   - Exodus 20:12

> [16] "Honor your father and your mother, as the LORD your God has commanded you, so that you may live long and that it may go well with you in the land the LORD your God is giving you.   - Deuteronomy 5:16

There are 8 references in the Bible to this commandment, 6 of which are in the New Testament. Does that suggest how important this is to God, not just your natural parents but spiritual ones as well? The Lord desires us to receive our inheritance freely as adopted children of our heavenly father through faithfulness, not as illegitimate children who attempt to steal someone else' inheritance. The previous example of Elijah and Elisha demonstrates the passing of the mantle to a true son of the faith, through inheritance and honoring the father.

Honor those who have gone before you, so that you may walk upon the path they paved with their blood, sweat and tears. What took them 20 years of their lives to carve out of the mountain could possibly only take you 6 months to assimilate into your life and then quickly build and expand upon the foundation they have laid. It is a New Testament principle. "Freely you have received, freely give." It is given by honoring your fathers and mothers, and receiving freely the impartation of the spiritual mantle and gifts they carry. Jesus gave good gifts to men, some of which are packaged in honorable vessels, the mentors and teachers that have trained and nurtured you.

> [8] Heal the sick, raise the dead, cleanse those who have leprosy, drive out demons. Freely you have received, freely give.
> - Matthew 10:8

The Fragrance of Death

> [15] Precious in the sight of the LORD is the death of his saints.   - Psalms 116:15

The word of God says that the death of his righteous ones is precious to Him, so when you honor their deaths (even though they are still alive and going through spiritual dying) you honor the Lord who deems it precious the fragrance their death has produced. And after all He is the only one who can bring life out of death (which is the seed that dies, goes into the ground and produces a harvest).

> [24] Verily, verily, I say unto you, Except a corn of wheat fall into the ground and die, it abideth alone: but if it die, it bringeth forth much fruit.   - John 12:24 KJV

The Scatterer of the Sheep

The enemy can sometimes come to sift your leader, or attack the shepherd. His goal is to scatter the sheep, or you, and to steal, kill, and destroy the work that the Lord has begun there. So don't rejoice when they are humiliated or sifted, pray for them, honor them, and bless them. Hold them up before the Father and let them know you appreciate them and stand with them. Also remember that Lucifer was the worship leader of Heaven, and he hates worship leaders because they are positionally standing where he used to stand. He wanted all the glory for himself. When you glorify the Lord you are giving unto the Lord what the enemy covets for himself.

The enemy doesn't want you to give any glory unto the Lord and so when the heat is on, sometimes you have to just buckle down and recognize the warfare. Draw from your spiritual armory which is high praises unto the Lord and worshipping the Lord so deeply, that you move Him. Where the Presence and the Radiance and the Glory of the Lord are, the enemy cannot stand to be. Want to move him out? Then move God in. Let your worship so move the Lord that He can't help but to draw closer and step foot on your property and come into your midst.

An Exercise in Harmony

One exercise in achieving true harmony and Biblical unity is to worship together and pray with one another outside of the church. Worship without microphones. Prefer one another. Enjoy the fragrance of one another's worship. When God can take you into another realm together, that experience and many others combined can create the most wonderful spiritual bond that the enemy cannot easily topple those God has assembled together. You also begin to learn one another's strengths, recognize when each is in the anointing, and learn how to support each other when the anointing has shifted between each of you. When you have a team that truly prefers one another, the Holy Spirit has ample opportunity to use each one of you to produce the most beautiful and harmonious rainbow of sound, color, and fragrance.

A Glorious Rainbow

This is what Heaven will truly be like. A rainbow has so many beautiful colors, no one more beautiful than the other, and they flow endlessly into one another. But the whole rainbow itself as a whole is truly breathtaking. Your worship can be a glorious rainbow that covers him who sits upon the Throne and rests upon him like the most wonderful blanket, one he loves to cuddle with. Be a part of that blanket, not the quilted square that stands out apart from the rest.

The Glory is His Alone

The Glory is his and his alone, don't touch it or want it for yourself. When you can be trusted to carry his Glory and keep your hands off of it, then you can be trusted to carry his Glory to the nations.

> [7] "Suppose one of you had a servant plowing or looking after the sheep. Would he say to the servant when he comes in from the field, 'Come along now and sit down to eat'? [8] Would he not rather say, 'Prepare my supper, get yourself ready and wait on me while I eat and drink; after that you may eat and drink'? [9] Would he thank the servant because he did what he was told to do? [10] So you also, when you have done everything you were told to do, should say, 'We are unworthy servants; we have only done our duty.' "
> — Luke 17:7-10

> [33] But seek ye first the kingdom of God, and his righteousness; and all these things shall be added unto you.
> — Matthew 6:33

Are you trustworthy with God?

In Ezekiel 44:10-16, Ezekiel is very explicit about who was able to come near to minister unto the Lord. God only allowed the sons of Zadok to come close enough to minister unto Him. The other Levites who were priests were forbidden to come near or minister unto the Lord because "...they performed their duties in the presence of their idols." The title of the hit show "American Idol" has a lot of truth in it. They are performing for the accolades of man. This is the world's version of worship. This is being done on church platforms all across America. The American Idol mentality has crept into worship teams, performing for man's approval, performing for the accolades of man, outdoing one another, fighting over mic time, singing over one another, performing to the camera, as unto Jesus. Forgive my harshness, but God is not impressed with our ability to perform. He has enough singers, instrumentalists, and performers who call what they do, worship. What impresses the heart of God is the worshipper that moves Him at His core, and refuses the praises of man for himself.

Where the Rubber Meets the Road

This is where the worshipper must come into a place of seeking personal deliverance for themselves. What is wounded in you that seeks the praises or approval of man? What need are you trying to fulfill by being on the platform or in front of people? This is the root of performance! What in you limits the fullness of God's Anointing and his Manifested Presence? At what level of maturity are you? These are tough questions and when we spend the time and due diligence with the Lord in private, he can heal us, restore us, tell us the truth, and prepare us to be holy, consecrated ministers and priests unto him.

We will find exponential blessing when we learn how to approach him in a way that truly honors him. And, the glory of the Lord will find praises that he may inhabit that lingers instead of visiting every once in a while.

It's Your Responsibility

Personal preparation is the responsibility of every worshipper through personal introspection. If you can yield to the Holy Spirit's guidance and the pruning of his knife you can come into compliance with him. This can be a quicker process than you think.

I have found the biggest obstacles to be pride and our not wanting to admit or even see some of the ugly things in our lives. Courage to face what he shows you while humbling yourself under his mighty hand, is instrumental in achieving his purposes. And, this is the part I already talked about; this is your path of dying daily. It is not for the fainthearted, but you ask for a hard thing. The Holy Spirit is a gentleman and he will not burden you with more than you can bear. He will gently lead you through this process. Now, you may smell like smoke when he's done with you, but you will not succumb to the flames. His strength will cover you in your weakness. The glory of Heaven awaits you here on earth. It will be but a light affliction compared to the surpassing greatness of his glory upon you and being shared through you. And his pleasure will be so sweet; he will be grinning from ear to ear, because your faith and your worship moved him at his core.

A Man or Woman after His Own Heart

You will be like David, a man or woman after his own heart. This chapter is waiting to be written in your own memoirs.

> 2 Let him kiss me with the kisses of his mouth— for your love is more delightful than wine.   - Song of Solomon 1:2

You cannot kiss him that he won't kiss you back. And when he kisses you, you know that you have been kissed! This is only the first chapter, but it is loaded with practical application and a mere introduction to some of the principles that will be discussed in greater detail later in the book. I believe through reading and assimilating these principles, there will be an impartation into your spirit, and you will see how these things will come alive in your life.

Chapter 2
Exposing the Political Platform

I want to introduce you to a biblical character very few even know about. His name is Absalom. This chapter is primarily written to expose some of the games that are currently being played and to some worship leaders, point out where they may already be in trouble but don't know it yet. You may sense that something is looming on the horizon. You can't quite put your finger on it but something is brooding. Your balloon may have already popped and you've seen that all that goes on behind the scene is not perfect. Everyone on the platform is an earthly being, made of flesh and many have untransformed areas of their soul that find an audience with the applause and accolades of man. This journey begins with where we are now to where the glory is. So hang on until we get there.

Lesson: God is preparing his priests to be holy and consecrated before him, and in making the Holy Spirit feel welcome, there are certain conditions that must be present. This is where I believe worldly ways have crept into the church and onto the worship platform. Prayerfully let the Holy Spirit show you if this is applicable or not in your ministry.

Where did Absalom come from?

Absalom was a son of the mighty King David, who was the humble and wholehearted psalmist. And you would think that music and devotion would run in the family, right? Let's read about him in the following passages:

> 2 Sons were born to David in Hebron: His firstborn was Amnon the son of Ahinoam of Jezreel; 3 his second, Kileab the son of Abigail the widow of Nabal of Carmel; the third, Absalom the son of Maacah daughter of Talmai king of Geshur; 4 the fourth, Adonijah the son of Haggith; the fifth, Shephatiah the son of Abital; 5 and the sixth, Ithream the son of David's wife Eglah. These were born to David in Hebron
> - 2 Samuel 3:2-5

David was the newly anointed King over Judah and moved to his first home in Hebron.

This was a time of war. Saul had lost his kingdom due to his own sin of idolatry (consulting
the witch of Endor) and took his own life after
losing his three sons on the battlefield with the
Philistines. Now besides the fact that David had
a lot of wives, as was the custom of the day,
David was also blessed with many children.
Not much is known about Absalom's mother
Maacah, but of her homeland Geshur, the people
were descendants of the inhabitants that were
not driven out of the land when Joshua and the
Israelites took over the land. In fact this is what
scripture says:

> **13 But the Israelites did not drive out the
> people of Geshur and Maacah, so they con-
> tinue to live among the Israelites to this
> day.   - Joshua 13:13.**

It's interesting that David's wife was
actually named after the other people that were
not driven out of the land. I believe the significance is that they were both represented here.
As was the custom, daughters of kings were
usually given as part of a treaty to ensure future
peace between nations and peoples. I believe by
marrying Maacah, David formed a political
alliance that set the stage for future events to
occur. Geshur was just northeast of the perime-
ter of Saul's kingdom, but later assimilated into

David's kingdom. Though scripture doesn't go into the specifics, I believe this merger of lands suggests that a treaty or at least a peaceful coexistence was formed by this union. In fact, of all the mothers listed, Maacah was the only one that was the daughter of a foreign king. Incidentally, this is during the period before the ark of the covenant came into David's remembrance. So I believe we have established that there are probably political roots involved with this alliance. Mothers tend to raise their children in the way they were raised, and probably in the customs and religious practices they grew up with. This marriage was an unequal yoking since there were to be none left in the land during Joshua's conquest, and in keeping with their Jewish customs they were not to commingle with other people, or assimilate their idolatrous practices.

[51] "Speak to the Israelites and say to them: 'When you cross the Jordan into Canaan, [52] drive out all the inhabitants of the land before you. Destroy all their carved images and their cast idols, and demolish all their high places. [53] Take possession of the land and settle in it, for I have given you the land to possess. - Numbers 33:51-53

Lesson: Because of disobedience to the Lord there was an open door. The sin may have not manifested itself immediately; the enemy obtained a legal right and waited for opportunity to exercise it. Knowing what has been on your land prior to your arrival to include any "open doors" is key to your cleansing the land. Submit to the Holy Spirit's leading who will guide you into all truth. Inquire of the Lord for revelation of what has existed prior to your arrival and repent on behalf of those who have gone before you. Close all the doors the Lord shows you, wipe the slate clean, and declare it holy ground unto the Lord.

Who is this character Absalom?

As we read in 2 Samuel 13, you will find the reappearance of Absalom. This passage gives insight into the heart of the man. As the story goes, Amnon, the firstborn of David, falls in love with Tamar, the sister of Absalom who was third in the line of succession, and whom was technically Amnon's stepsister. Upon listening to improper advice, Amnon pretends to be ill and asks his father David to send Tamar, his sister to feed him. Amnon then rapes her and is disgusted with her, sending her away disgraced. Tamar then goes to live in her brother Absalom's house as a desolate woman. King David was furious but scripture does not record any further discipline.

22 Absalom never said a word to Amnon, either good or bad; he hated Amnon because he had disgraced his sister Tamar.

- 2 Samuel 13:22

As you can see, hatred, anger, bitterness, and revenge began to take root in Absalom's heart. Offense was the open door, and things weren't handled with repentance, forgiveness or correction, according to scripture. Two years later Absalom devises a scheme to invite his father and brothers to a "Sheepherders' Convention". His father David doesn't want to go but gives his blessing to Absalom.

26 Then Absalom said, "If not, please let my brother Amnon come with us." The king asked him, "Why should he go with you?"

27 But Absalom urged him, so he sent with him Amnon and the rest of the king's sons.

28 Absalom ordered his men, "Listen! When Amnon is in high spirits from drinking wine and I say to you, 'Strike Amnon down,' then

kill him. Don't be afraid. Have not I given you this order? Be strong and brave." 29 So Absalom's men did to Amnon what Absalom had ordered. Then all the king's sons got up, mounted their mules and fled.

- 2 Samuel 13:26-29

Did David just not have a clue as to what was in the heart of his son Absalom? He did question why Amnon should go with Absalom, yet he did not trust his gut instinct as to Absalom's intentions. At first, sketchy details come back to the king and it is first reported that all the king's sons were killed by Absalom. Later the truth is learned that only Amnon, firstborn of David was killed.

32 But Jonadab son of Shimeah, David's brother, said, "My lord should not think that they killed all the princes; only Amnon is dead. This has been Absalom's expressed intention ever since the day Amnon raped his sister Tamar.

33 My lord the king should not be concerned about the report that all the king's sons are dead. Only Amnon is dead." 34 Meanwhile, Absalom had fled.   - 2 Samuel 13:32-34

And guess where Absalom fled?

³⁷ Absalom fled and went to Talmai son of Ammihud, the king of Geshur. But King David mourned for his son every day. ³⁸ After Absalom fled and went to Geshur, he stayed there three years. ³⁹ And the spirit of the king longed to go to Absalom, for he was consoled concerning Amnon's death.

- 2 Samuel 13:37-39

So Absalom went back to his mother's homeland of Geshur to the house of his grandfather. Who knows what all went on there! We can only speculate.

Lesson: Having your house in order is extremely critical when you're in frontline ministry. And believe me, worship ministry is a frontline ministry. This is important for the worship leader as well as worship team members. I myself have taken time off in order to get things in my own family in order. God always honors those who first take care of their family. In the process of closing doors and preparing your family, the anointing and presence of God will increase in your life and your ministry. Don't lose your family on the altar of ministry. That is not a pleasing sacrifice unto God.

The Return of Absalom

> ¹ Joab son of Zeruiah knew that the king's heart longed for Absalom. ² So Joab sent someone to Tekoa and had a wise woman brought from there. He said to her, "Pretend you are in mourning. Dress in mourning clothes, and don't use any cosmetic lotions. Act like a woman who has spent many days grieving for the dead. ³ Then go to the king and speak these words to him." And Joab put the words in her mouth.
>
> - 2 Samuel 14:1-3

Now Joab, which was David's commander and right hand man, knew how much David loved and longed for his son Absalom. So in verses 4-20, Joab devises a plan to bring back Absalom. In doing so Joab solicits the help of a wise woman, an actress, to reenact the drama of David and his wayfaring son.

> ¹¹ She said, "Then let the king invoke the LORD his God to prevent the avenger of blood from adding to the destruction, so that my son will not be destroyed." "As surely as the LORD lives," he said, "not one hair of your son's head will fall to the ground."
>
> - 2 Samuel 14:11

When David gives his verdict on the wise woman's behalf, the truth that this was really all about David comes forth, and that Joab put her up to it. So David relents and allows his son Absalom to return to Jerusalem.

> ²¹ **The king said to Joab, "Very well, I will do it. Go, bring back the young man Absalom."** ²³ **Then Joab went to Geshur and brought Absalom back to Jerusalem.** ²⁴ **But the king said, "He must go to his own house; he must not see my face." So Absalom went to his own house and did not see the face of the king.** - 2 Samuel 14:21, 23-24

Lesson: There must be restoration before returning to the worship platform. This is especially true when a breach in relationship, mistakes, or open sin has occurred. Reconciliation and evidence that a change of the heart has occurred in their life is very important. A person with open doors or sin in their life will bring these issues to the worship platform and to the team.

The Word of God makes a little side note here that I believe is very significant. It appears to be off the sequence of the story; a little background info.

> [25] In all Israel there was not a man so highly praised for his handsome appearance as Absalom. From the top of his head to the sole of his foot there was no blemish in him. [26]Whenever he cut the hair of his head—he used to cut his hair from time to time when it became too heavy for him—he would weigh it, and its weight was two hundred shekels [about 5 pounds] by the royal standard.
>
> - 2 Samuel 14:25-26

Absalom was beautiful, charismatic, and captivating in his appearance and demeanor. He was probably very charming, well educated and well mannered, as the son of a King. And he probably flashed a beautiful smile which melted the heart of any woman and won the admiration of his peers.

This was a guy who looked like he had it all together. As royalty, he probably had the clothes, the family, and the beautiful house. But remember when we previously looked into the heart of the man we saw offense, resentment, bitterness, and murder. All was not as it appeared. He also quietly schemed for two years to kill his oldest brother.

Lesson: Someone joining your team may appear to be put together, charismatic and attractive, out sing other team members, have great ideas or possess multiple talents and abilities that are needed on the team. But they have underlying agendas or motives waiting to be exercised. God does not always choose the most talented nor the most charismatic or attractive people through which to operate. Sometimes God chooses the person man would not choose, the one with a pure heart. Look for their fruit and you will know who and whose they are. If they bring strife, division, insurrection, manipulation and control or rebellion, these things are not of God and they will destroy the work of the ministry. God has his "sent ones". The enemy can infiltrate your camp with his. Know the hearts of the people you are ministering with. Do not promote people because of their talent, abilities, or potential, and certainly not before they are ready. Their talent may have gotten them on the team, but their character will prove them and keep them there. Let the Holy Spirit show you with whom you are co-laboring.

Absalom gains entrance with the King

²⁸ Absalom lived two years in Jerusalem without seeing the king's face. ²⁹ Then Absalom sent for Joab in order to send him to the king, but Joab refused to come to him. So he sent a second time, but he refused to come. ³⁰ Then he said to his servants, "Look, Joab's field is next to mine, and he has barley there. Go and set it on fire." So Absalom's servants set the field on fire.

³¹ Then Joab did go to Absalom's house and he said to him, "Why have your servants set my field on fire?" ³² Absalom said to Joab, "Look, I sent word to you and said, 'Come here so I can send you to the king to ask, "Why have I come from Geshur? It would be better for me if I were still there!" 'Now then, I want to see the king's face, and if I am guilty of anything, let him put me to death."

³³ So Joab went to the king and told him this. Then the king summoned Absalom, and he came in and bowed down with his face to the ground before the king. And the king kissed Absalom.   - 2 Samuel 14: 28-33

Absalom becomes impatient with his circumstances and he calls up Joab. When Joab will not see him, he sets his fields on fire. Is this not a spoiled child having a temper tantrum and trying to manipulate to get his own way? Now you might bring up the fact that Joab used manipulation first. But remember manipulation comes from the heart. The scripture reflects that Joab was sensitive to the heart of David, and out of his genuine concern for David, brought him to a place where he could be reunited with his son. David loved his son Absalom, Joab loved his king, David, but look at Absalom's request in verse 32.

> ³² Absalom said to Joab, "Look, I sent word to you and said, 'Come here so I can send you to the king to ask, "Why have I come from Geshur? It would be better for me if I were still there!" 'Now then, I want to see the king's face, and if I am guilty of any- thing, let him put me to death."
> - 2 Samuel 14:32

Love is not at the heart of Absalom's request. In fact an agenda could have already been brewing in him, even while he was living in David's country for two years, and three years previously at his grandfather's house. There is no repentance in his request, only a desire to see the king, and to see him now! When Absalom is finally presented to the king, he knows how to approach him and he bows down with his face to the ground before the king. David, his father, kissed him, for in his heart he had longed for this day, a time to be reunited with his son. Of course Absalom knew of his father's compassionate heart concerning him and he was counting on this type of reception. Now it may seem that I am being a little harsh on this guy, but let's see what's just around the corner.

Absalom's Conspiracy

¹ In the course of time, Absalom provided himself with a chariot and horses and with fifty men to run ahead of him. ² He would get up early and stand by the side of the road leading to the city gate. Whenever anyone came with a complaint to be placed before the king for a decision, Absalom would call out to him, "What town are you from?" He would answer, "Your servant is from one of the tribes of Israel."

³ Then Absalom would say to him, "Look, your claims are valid and proper, but there is no representative of the king to hear you." ⁴ And Absalom would add, "If only I were appointed judge in the land! Then everyone who has a complaint or case could come to me and I would see that he gets justice." ⁵ Also, whenever anyone approached him to

bow down before him, Absalom would reach out his hand, take hold of him and kiss him.

6 Absalom behaved in this way toward all the Israelites who came to the king asking for justice, and so he stole the hearts of the men of Israel.   - 2 Samuel 15:1-6

Where did this come from? This parallels our modern day politics. Absalom would stand on the side of the road waiting for someone to come with a complaint or a problem, and he would intercept them on their way to the King. After all he was royalty, and he seemed to really care about the people and their problems.

> **4 And Absalom would add, "If only I were appointed judge in the land! Then everyone who has a complaint or case could come to me and I would see that he gets justice."**
> - 2 Samuel 15:4

If you elect me as judge I will put an end to injustice and rule in your favor! If I were the leader, I would go to bat for you. I would see that things are done right and all your problems would go away. First, Absalom circumvented the chain of authority. Second, he was promoting himself and his agenda. Third, he was coveting their votes, and actively pursuing the voters. Absalom was out, "shaking hands and kissing babies." It sounds kind of like he was going "door to door" with a brochure in hand. Do you see the politics here? All he had to do was flash that winning smile and turn on his charismatic charm and he had them. I am not against Christians being public servants or being involved in the political process. As a matter of fact, I believe Christians should effect change in their government and stand for Godly principles in order to safeguard their beliefs and to ensure peace in their land for future generations. But there's more here than meets the eye.

> ⁵ Also, whenever anyone approached him to bow down before him, Absalom would reach out his hand, take hold of him and kiss him. ⁶ Absalom behaved in this way toward all the Israelites who came to the king asking for justice, and so he stole the hearts of the men of Israel.   - 2 Samuel 15:5-6

Absalom, the prince, was accustomed to royal treatment. As the son of the King, the people would bow and show him honor due his title. But here he forgoes the normal accolades, and does not allow them to bow, appearing to them that they have equal footing with him. Their "equality" to the prince gives them a false sense of promotion but there are strings attached. He is winning political favor with all the men of Israel, and so it says that he "...stole the hearts of the men of Israel." Have you ever seen this before? It may even begin with flattery or a sense of equality until the trump card is pulled. Everyone wants to be with the popular guy.

The Trump Card is Pulled

7 At the end of four years, Absalom said to the king, "Let me go to Hebron and fulfill a vow I made to the LORD. 8 While your servant was living at Geshur in Aram, I made this vow: 'If the LORD takes me back to Jerusalem, I will worship the LORD in Hebron. ' "

9 The king said to him, "Go in peace." So he went to Hebron. 10 Then Absalom sent secret messengers throughout the tribes of Israel to say, "As soon as you hear the sound of the trumpets, then say, 'Absalom is king in Hebron." 11 <u>Two hundred men from Jerusalem had accompanied Absalom. They had been invited as guests and went quite innocently, knowing nothing about the matter.</u>

12 While Absalom was offering sacrifices, he also sent for Ahithophel the Gilonite, David's counselor, to come from Giloh, his hometown. <u>And so the conspiracy gained</u>

All the political maneuvering and winning of the hearts of the men has now come with a price tag. The agenda, hidden for years is now revealed. What seemed to be offered freely now proves to be quite expensive. We're talking about overthrowing the kingdom, setting up the throne of Absalom, and eventually going after the very life of King David, his own father. I don't think the men of Israel signed up for that. But once they had given their loyalty to Absalom they were forced to pay up in full. They probably loved their beloved King David but they had come into alignment with the very opposition that intended to set up its own throne and oust the king no matter the cost.

The root of all this is found in the motivations of Absalom's heart. First of all, he was impatient and made things happen by his own power instead of waiting on God. He used every trick in the book including lying, manipulation, slander, backbiting, and flattery. He also relied on his charm, charisma, talents, abilities, etc. to accomplish his own will which was to set up his own throne instead of inheriting the throne by promise. Essentially Absalom was jealous of his own father and envied what his father had, the position, throne, power, admiration of the people, and the very place God had given him. He was willing to accomplish his will by political maneuvering, a coup d'etat to overthrow the kingdom, betrayal, conspiracy, and even murder. He resorted to self promotion instead of Godly promotion. And once he stole the hearts of the men and they unknowingly aligned with him, they came against the king God had set upon the throne, the man after God's own heart, the sweet psalmist of Israel, the champion of Israel, the one Samuel had crowned king, the one whose house and throne would reign forever.

One may ask how this could happen to such a good man. Let's look at how he responded to the heartbreaking news of his son's ultimate betrayal.

David's Response

> [13] A messenger came and told David, "The hearts of the men of Israel are with Absalom." [14] Then David said to all his officials who were with him in Jerusalem, "Come! We must flee, or none of us will escape from Absalom. We must leave immediately, or he will move quickly to overtake us and bring ruin upon us and put the city to the sword."

¹⁵ The king's officials answered him, "Your servants are ready to do whatever our lord the king chooses." ¹⁶ The king set out, with his entire household following him; but he left ten concubines to take care of the palace. ¹⁷ So the king set out, with all the people following him, and they halted at a place some distance away. ¹⁸ All his men marched past him, along with all the Kerethites and Pelethites; and all the six hundred Gittites who had accompanied him from Gath marched before the king.

¹⁹ The king said to Ittai the Gittite, "Why should you come along with us? Go back and stay with King Absalom. You are a foreigner, an exile from your homeland. ²⁰ You came only yesterday. And today shall I make you wander about with us, when I do not know where I am going? Go back, and take your countrymen. May kindness and faithfulness be with you." ²¹ But Ittai replied to the king, "As surely as the LORD lives, and as my lord the king lives, wherever my lord the king may be, whether it means life or death, there will your servant be." ²² David said to Ittai, "Go ahead, march on." So Ittai the Gittite marched on with all his men and the families that were with him.

²³ The whole countryside wept aloud as all the people passed by. The king also crossed the Kidron Valley, and all the people moved

on toward the desert. [24] Zadok was there, too, and all the Levites who were with him were carrying the ark of the covenant of God. They set down the ark of God, and Abiathar offered sacrifices until all the people had finished leaving the city. [25] Then the king said to Zadok, "Take the ark of God back into the city. If I find favor in the LORD's eyes, he will bring me back and let me see it and his dwelling place again. [26] But if he says, 'I am not pleased with you,' then I am ready; let him do to me whatever seems good to him."

[27] The king also said to Zadok the priest, "Aren't you a seer? Go back to the city in peace, with your son Ahimaaz and Jonathan son of Abiathar. You and Abiathar take your two sons with you. [28] I will wait at the fords in the desert until word comes from you to inform me." [29] So Zadok and Abiathar took the ark of God back to Jerusalem and stayed there.

[30] But David continued up the Mount of Olives, weeping as he went; his head was covered and he was barefoot. All the people with him covered their heads too and were weeping as they went up. [31] Now David had been told, "Ahithophel is among the conspirators with Absalom." So David prayed, "O LORD, turn Ahithophel's counsel into foolishness." [32] When David arrived at the

summit, where people used to worship God, Hushai the Arkite was there to meet him, his robe torn and dust on his head.

33 David said to him, "If you go with me, you will be a burden to me. 34 But if you return to the city and say to Absalom, 'I will be your servant, O king; I was your father's servant in the past, but now I will be your servant,' then you can help me by frustrating Ahithophel's advice. 35 Won't the priests Zadok and Abiathar be there with you? Tell them anything you hear in the king's palace. 36 Their two sons, Ahimaaz son of Zadok and Jonathan son of Abiathar, are there with them. Send him to me with anything you hear." 37 So David's friend Hushai arrived at Jerusalem as Absalom was entering the city

- 2 Samuel 15:13-37

I was tempted to give just a few verses here, but this entire passage really shows David's heart. And, even though he was the king the man truly walked in humility. He could have stayed and fought for his kingdom and his throne. After all God was on his side. There were many other battles where he asked the Lord if he should fight, and the Lord instructed him to fight, thus winning the battle. Why not here? He was sitting in the place and position to which God had called him, he was anointed by God to be king. He was God's first choice as King, he worshipped God like no other, and he stood up to Goliath as Israel's champion. If there was ever a time where he would be justified in fighting for what was rightfully his, given by God, this would have been that time. There was much weeping, the people didn't want to see him go, David wept aloud, leaving everything God had given him in verses 23 and 30. He even took the ark which carried the presence of God, with him. But, later he told Zadok and the priests to return to the city with the ark. When Absalom took over the city, he would then have the ark, which represented the anointing and the presence of God, in his possession. David leaves everything in the hands of the one who put him there. Look what he says:

> 25 Then the king said to Zadok, "Take the ark of God back into the city. If I find favor in the LORD's eyes, he will bring me back and let me see it and his dwelling place again. 26 But if he says, 'I am not pleased with you,' then I am ready; let him do to me whatever seems good to him."
>
> - 2 Samuel 15:25-26.

Is this not the epitome of trust? He trusted in the one who put him in his position, so much that he was willing to leave it all and let God decide. He didn't even try to defend himself, his throne, position, or kingdom. David even sent back the ark of the Lord's presence, anointing and glory back to where it had been. He even allowed it to be placed into the hands of the one who betrayed him. (That's a hard thing to see the anointing and glory remain, even when you are forced to leave it along with your blessing.) David wore the mantle of humility. I can't help but see the prophetic parallel of Jesus as he left it all and went to the cross, even though his kingdom was seemingly being overthrown and taken over by another.

> [30] But David continued up the Mount of Olives, weeping as he went; his head was covered and he was barefoot.
>
> - 2 Samuel 15:30

Consider this passage in Philippians 2:1-11

> [1] If you have any encouragement from being united with Christ, if any comfort from his love, if any fellowship with the Spirit, if any tenderness and compassion, [2] then make my joy complete by being like-minded, having the same love, being one in spirit and

purpose. 3 Do nothing out of selfish ambition or vain conceit, but in humility, consider others better than yourselves. 4 Each of you should look not only to your own interests, but also to the interests of others. 5 Your attitude should be the same as that of Christ Jesus: 6 Who, being in very nature God, did not consider equality with God something to be grasped,

7 but made himself nothing, taking the very nature of a servant, being made in human likeness. 8 And being found in appearance as a man, he humbled himself and became obedient to death— even death on a cross! 9 Therefore God exalted him to the highest place and gave him the name that is above every name, 10 that at the name of Jesus every knee should bow, in heaven and on earth and under the earth, 11 and every tongue confess that Jesus Christ is Lord, to the glory of God the Father.

- Philippians 2:1-11

I believe David's trust so moved the Hand of God that the burden of responsibility was now in God's lap. David walked a road of humiliation, sorrow, and unspeakable grief. He didn't know what hit him, and certainly had no plans for the future or even what to do with the cards that he had been dealt. This was certainly not the outcome he expected from his calling to be king. He was even cursed at and spit upon by some of his own people.

> [5] As King David approached Bahurim, a man from the same clan as Saul's family came out from there. His name was Shimei son of Gera, and he cursed as he came out. [6] He pelted David and all the king's officials with stones, though all the troops and the special guard were on David's right and left. [7] As he cursed, Shimei said, "Get out, get out, you man of blood, you scoundrel! [8] The LORD has repaid you for all the blood you shed in the household of Saul, in whose place you have reigned. The LORD has handed the kingdom over to your son Absalom. You have come to ruin because you are a man of blood!"   - 2 Samuel 15:5-8

Lesson: False judgment was passed over David, in a gleeful fashion. Sure David was called to war, but God was not the one bringing forth judgment upon him. This was definitely the work of the enemy to kill, steal, and destroy David. Be very careful when you feel the temptation to rejoice when others, especially leaders, are in a time of suffering. They may not be paying a "penance" for a wrong doing. The enemy may be coming after them with

a vengeance due to the threat they pose to
him by what they are doing right.

Where is God in all this?

> [14] Absalom and all the men of Israel said,
> "The advice of Hushai the Arkite is better
> than that of Ahithophel." <u>For the LORD had
> determined to frustrate the good advice of
> Ahithophel in order to bring disaster on Ab-
> salom.</u>   - 2 Samuel 17:14

David still had men loyal to him, one of
which was his good friend Hushai the Arkite.
David sent him back into Absalom's house,
available to be used by God. The Lord is definitely working behind the scenes to frustrate the
work of the enemy. Hushai then sends a mes-
sage through Zadok, the loyal priest sent back
to the city, to David letting him know of Absalom's plans to find and kill David.

> [31] Now David had been told, "Ahithophel is
> among the conspirators with Absalom." So
> David prayed, "O LORD, turn Ahithophel's
> counsel into foolishness." [32] When David ar-
> rived at the summit, where people used to
> worship God, Hushai the Arkite was there to
> meet him, his robe torn and dust on his

head. ³³ David said to him, "If you go with me, you will be a burden to me.

³⁴ But if you return to the city and say to Absalom, 'I will be your servant, O king; I was your father's servant in the past, but now I will be your servant,' then you can help me by frustrating Ahithophel's advice.

³⁵ Won't the priests Zadok and Abiathar be there with you? Tell them anything you hear in the king's palace. ³⁶ Their two sons, Ahimaaz son of Zadok and Jonathan son of Abiathar, are there with them. Send them to me with anything you hear." ³⁷ So David's friend Hushai arrived at Jerusalem as Absalom was entering the city.
- 2 Samuel 15:13-37

David did not have a clue how to fix this situation. In the midst of the crisis, he first prayed, and then being the king he was, he issued orders. God did everything according to the orders and the plan David decreed. God did not even circumvent the authority of his anointed one, King David. Is God not a God of order? He operated through his own authority placed in David, and did everything according to David's plea. Quite frankly, the Holy Spirit probably gave him the supernatural path, the way of escape, and David being sensitive to the Spirit of God tapped into God's creative plan of restoration. God could have created a new and inventive method to restore David, but He chose to restore David through the authority of David's prayer and his kingly decree.

> *Lesson:* When you find yourself broadsided by the enemy, your quiet prayer and plea for God's help may result in your issuing a kingly decree with your appointed authority, instead of declaring your circumstance. Heaven comes into agreement with the kingly decree issued; instead of you coming into agreement with the circumstance. When you don't know what to do, put your best foot forward, in faith, knowing that God has already promised that He would order your steps, and let God lead you by his Holy Spirit. God may want to teach you how much authority you really have and how you can walk above your circumstances into victory.

David then gives orders to his men concerning his son Absalom.

> ⁵ **The king commanded Joab, Abishai and Ittai, "Be gentle with the young man Absalom for my sake." And all the troops heard the king giving orders concerning Absalom to each of the commanders. - 2 Samuel 18:5**

Love truly is the more excellent way. David's heart is to love his enemy, even if it is his own son, and to turn the other cheek. He is really operating by New Testament principles, because this is not according to the laws of his day, especially when dealing with a traitor and betrayer of a king. God couldn't help but honor this man who operated by the rule of love. Consider these scriptures.

> 12 Hatred stirs up dissension, but love covers over all wrongs.   Proverbs 10:12

> 9 He who covers over an offense promotes love, but whoever repeats the matter separates close friends.   - Proverbs 17:9

> 8Above all, love each other deeply, because love covers over a multitude of sins.
>   - 1 Peter 4:8

Absalom's Demise

> [9] Now Absalom happened to meet David's men. He was riding his mule, and as the mule went under the thick branches of a large oak, <u>Absalom's head got caught in the tree. He was left hanging in midair, while the mule he was riding kept on going.</u> [10] When one of the men saw this, he told Joab,

"I just saw Absalom hanging in an oak tree."
11 Joab said to the man who had told him
this, "What! You saw him? Why didn't you
strike him to the ground right there? Then I
would have had to give you ten shekels of
silver and a warrior's belt."

12 But the man replied, "Even if a thousand
shekels were weighed out into my hands, I
would not lift my hand against the king's
son. In our hearing the king commanded you
and Abishai and Ittai, 'Protect the young
man Absalom for my sake.' 13 And if I had
put my life in jeopardy —and nothing is
hidden from the king—you would have kept
your distance from me."

14 Joab said, "I'm not going to wait like this
for you." So he took three javelins in his
hand and plunged them into Absalom's
heart while Absalom was still alive in the
oak tree. 15 And ten of Joab's armor-bearers
surrounded Absalom, struck him and killed
him.

16 Then Joab sounded the trumpet, and the
troops stopped pursuing Israel, for Joab
halted them. 17 They took Absalom, threw
him into a big pit in the forest and piled up
a large heap of rocks over him. Meanwhile,
all the Israelites fled to their homes.

18 During his lifetime Absalom had taken a
pillar and erected it in the King's Valley as a
monument to himself, for he thought, "I

have no son to carry on the memory of my name." He named the pillar after himself, and it is called Absalom's Monument to this day.   - 2 Samuel 18:9-18

Do you remember the verdict that King David issued on behalf of the wise woman who Joab sent in order to bring Absalom back?

11 She said, "Then let the king invoke the LORD his God to prevent the avenger of blood from adding to the destruction, so that my son will not be destroyed." "As surely as the LORD lives," he said, "not one hair of your son's head will fall to the ground."
                                    - 2 Samuel 14:11

Isn't it interesting that Absalom's head got stuck in a tree? God even allowed the death of Absalom to be in accordance with the previous issue decreed, in that not one hair of Absalom fell to the ground, he was killed hanging in a tree. Now the fear of God is really coming upon me. The power of life and death is truly in the tongue.

21Death and life are in the power of the tongue: and they that love it shall eat the fruit thereof.   - Proverbs 18:21

And thus began David's journey back to his throne, though he mourned the death and demise of his own son, he reclaimed everything God had given him. One last side note:

> [18] During his lifetime Absalom had taken a pillar and erected it in the King's Valley as a monument to himself, for he thought, "I have no son to carry on the memory of my name." He named the pillar after himself, and it is called Absalom's Monument to this day. - 2 Samuel 18:18

I believe the Holy Spirit wants to caution us in erecting a pillar or monument in our own image, in the guise of ministry. Even the works of our own hands can become an idol, "Look what we have done!"

Sometimes God has to illuminate any places we have erected as idols in our own lives because he is a jealous God. Not even ministry or something he entrusted to you shall come before him. Take a private moment before the Lord and survey the landscape of your ministry. Inspect the works of your own hands. If there be any "high places," surrender them and repent before the Lord. I would rather know this side of Heaven that my life's work would survive the fire and come out as pure gold or silver, than to watch them later be reduced to ashes with no chance for redemption. God knows that we are on a giant learning curve, and sometimes the greatest wisdom comes from learning from the mistakes of others. Now that I have finished my private moment with the Lord, let's move on.

So, what does all this mean?

This has been an interesting bible study, but how does this apply to the ministry or the worship ministry specifically? Let's take a look at one more parallel, this time from the world. See if this is familiar.

A Parallel to a Worldly Dimension

Let's imagine that you have been hired to work in an office. At first your boss seems to have it all together, creative ideas, synergy, and rapport with the people. There seems to be unity in the office, and a lot is accomplished. One day a newbie is hired. This one has her eyes on the boss' job. She is charismatic and seems to "really care" about her coworkers, patting them on the back, going out of her way to make others feel good about their work. She may even engage in some back office gossip and complaining about the boss.

Pretty soon, dissatisfaction begins to surface, and little fires start burning. She may even begin to dialogue with the boss' boss and start to question the capabilities of the boss. Meanwhile she has gained the trust and favor of the other coworkers, and eventually what seemed to work in the past, no longer seems to make sense in the majority's opinion.

She has already begun an uprising, though not terribly obvious to the boss. Then something happens (and it always does!) that calls to question the competence of the boss and all the work that they have done. Enough groundwork has been laid and evidence gathered to convict the boss (though he may be completely innocent) and pretty soon someone is up for promotion (due to the newly vacated office of the boss, who had no clue what hit him). Who seems to be the most qualified to fill the position? You guessed it.

We have seen these worldly scenarios played out from soap operas to hospital shows, from "Law and Order" to "Dallas." This is the stereotypical "scratching your way to the top." It begins with violating the eighth, ninth, and tenth commandments.

¹⁵ "You shall not steal. ¹⁶ "You shall not give false testimony against your neighbor. ¹⁷ "You shall not covet your neighbor's house. You shall not covet your neighbor's wife, or his manservant or maidservant, his ox or donkey, or anything that belongs to your neighbor."   - Exodus 20:15-17

Now we don't expect the world to obey God's commandments, except as legislated by the government, but this is the church and God's people are supposed to know the Word of God concerning these things. These kinds of games are being played in ministries. The root is usually coveting, which breeds jealousy and envy, of talents, abilities, place, position, favor, ministry, by using many of the other tools of manipulation already covered. This may be such a subtle thing, and no one knows what is just around the corner.

I believe when the people of God expose the hidden agenda and schemes of the enemy, they are empowered with the means by which to fight the enemy to his ultimate defeat. Through the knowledge of God's word, and humble hearts who submit to God, repentance and forgiveness can bring forth a harvest of righteousness and the fruit of holiness. And those who dare to press into God, may find they are being transformed from glory to glory, and see a newness and freshness of God breathed into their ministry with a greater anointing.

And what is it that we are longing to see? We hunger for God's glory manifested in unprecedented ways through our worship on the platforms all across the landscape of the church. God is as interested in what is done behind the scenes as what is portrayed in front of the people in his sanctuary. God desires to clean his house, not to punish his people with harshness, so that he can bring a greater manifestation of his glory to a place where his holiness reigns. His glory cannot be separated from his holiness, and it is his grace that he refrains from visiting us with that level of glory, until we come up the mountain a little higher and can be sustained in the visitation.

> 3 Who may ascend the hill of the LORD? Who may stand in his holy place? 4 He who has clean hands and a pure heart, who does not lift up his soul to an idol or swear by what is false. 5 He will receive blessing from the LORD and vindication from God his Savior.   - Psalm 24:3-5

And that is a promise you can take to the Bank!

Chapter 3
The Fall of Pride

Lesson from one worship leader:

There are two worship leaders I want to explore that are mentioned in the Bible. I believe they have pertinent lessons for us as we explore the ministry of worship. The first one was the worship leader of heaven before he fell. According to the research and writings of Ray Hughes, Lucifer (Hebrew for Morning Star) was one of the cherubim that covered the throne and he was beautiful in appearance, having the very essence of all musical instrumentation in his very being, Isaiah 14:11. Can you imagine the beauty that he must have had and the music that exuded from him in heavenly orchestration, and the glory that must have surrounded him as he worshipped the Lord? However something was found in him. Let's see:

> [11] **All your pomp has been brought down to the grave, along with the noise of your harps;**

maggots are spread out beneath you
and worms cover you.

[12] How you have fallen from heaven,
O morning star, son of the dawn!
You have been cast down to the earth,
you who once laid low the nations!

[13] You said in your heart,
"I will ascend to heaven;
I will raise my throne
above the stars of God;
I will sit enthroned on the mount of assembly,
on the utmost heights of the sacred mountain.

[14] I will ascend above the tops of the clouds;
I will make myself like the Most High."

[15] But you are brought down to the grave,
to the depths of the pit. - Isaiah 14:12-15

The "I wills" of the Bible were found here in Lucifer's heart. Pride was found in him, and he wanted a portion of God's glory for himself. We have to be careful when handling God's glory, that we not touch it or skim off a portion for ourselves. Do you ever wonder why there is such warfare around the worship ministry, especially the worship leader? I believe it is because the worship leader is standing in that place that the enemy used to occupy, and I believe he still wants a portion of the glory, or at least for the glory to be given anywhere else except for the Lord himself. Let's look closer at the "I wills."

"I will Ascend..."

The first one is "I will ascend..." Have you ever imagined the thought of stardom, or a rising star? Or have you thought about you or your worship ministry rising in prominence in your city or your region? Or have you imagined the idea of rising in fame or being heard around the world through various recordings, venues, etc. We have to be vigilant against the "American Idol" mentality that has crept onto worship platforms across America. Once formed in your mind, these vain imaginations are the fertile soil where pride begins to take root in your heart. Jesus also fought this temptation with the word of God when Satan tempted him the third time in the wilderness.

> [8] Again, the devil took him to a very high mountain and showed him all the kingdoms of the world and their splendor. [9] "All this I will give you," he said, "if you will bow down and worship me."

[10] Jesus said to him, "Away from me, Satan! For it is written: 'Worship the Lord your God, and serve him only.'

[11] Then the devil left him, and angels came and attended him.   - Matthew 4:8-11

It is hard to imagine the devil's audacity to have even suggested the Lord Jesus bow down and worship him. Jesus used the word of God to conquer the religious spirit. Think about it. There are just two to be worshipped. It is either the Lord, or the religious spirit who was Satan himself who owned all other forms of religion as shown in, verses 8-9.

[8] "Again, the devil took him to a very high mountain and showed him all the kingdoms of the world and their splendor. [9] "All this I will give you," he said, "if you will bow down and worship me." - Matthew 4:8-9

He would rather take any praise or glory, even if it is not directly linked to him, in disguise than for the worship to be given to the Lord. He will even allow you to be put on a pedestal, to be idolized and to be worshipped. This is idolatry. It does not glorify God, it glorifies you, and as worship leaders we must be diligent to avoid this pitfall in our ministries.

"I will raise my throne..."

The second one is "I will raise my throne..." This is self promotion, and usually steps on the authorities that are already in place over you. It is demonstrated in a desire to out shine, to stand out, to out perform, or to belittle those around you so that you will rise to the top. This is exactly what Absalom did. He expressed his vain imaginations, "If only I were appointed judge in the land..." Later he amassed such a following of allies or "worshippers" who were willing to overthrow beloved King David and his kingdom to set up this false throne, illegitimately obtained through political schemes.

When we remember that God is our promoter, he will exalt us in due season, if we don't faint. When? It is when our character is mature enough in his eyes that it will not destroy us when we obtain his blessings and the fulfillment of our destinies in God.

The root of this self promotion is coveting that which is not ours or has been given to us by God. We resort to the manipulations of the flesh to get what we want. David gave us a clue in honoring those in authority.

¹⁵ "Do not touch my anointed ones;
do my prophets no harm." - Psalm 105:15

If we will ask of the Lord only that which he has reserved for us, and rejoice when God blesses others, we will safeguard our promotion and our right standing with Him. If God didn't give it to us, we don't want it anyway.

"I will sit enthroned..."

The third one is, "I will sit enthroned..." Who is enthroned in your heart? And who is enthroned on your worship platform? Sometimes our very ministries can take the place of the Lord on the throne of our hearts.

¹⁴ Do not worship any other god, for the LORD, whose name is Jealous, is a jealous God.   - Exodus 34:14

⁵⁸ They angered him with their high places; they aroused his jealousy with their idols
  - Psalm 78:58

As you can see he is a jealous God and he will not share his glory with anyone, not even you. Look at how Jesus thought of himself in Philippians 2, specifically in verses 5-8.

³ Do nothing out of selfish ambition or vain conceit, but in humility consider others better than yourselves.

⁴ Each of you should look not only to your own interests, but also to the interests of others. ⁵ Your attitude should be the same as that of Christ Jesus: ⁶ Who, being in very nature God, did not consider equality with God something to be grasped,

⁷ but made himself nothing,
taking the very nature of a servant,
being made in human likeness.
⁸ And being found in appearance as a man,
he humbled himself and became obedient to
death— even death on a cross!
⁹ Therefore God exalted him to the highest place and gave him the name that is above every name, ¹⁰ that at the name of Jesus every knee should bow, in heaven and on earth and under the earth,

¹¹ and every tongue confess that Jesus Christ is Lord, to the glory of God the Father.
- Philippians 2:3-11

Before Jesus was exalted, even though he was God, his humility preceded his exaltation, not by man but by God himself. Jesus is the example of how we are to allow the Father to promote us into our destiny. God exalted him to the very highest place. We should be in the same likeness as Christ and do things in the proper way. In due season, the building of character and then the fruit of humility will lead to your promotion. When God exalts, it is known by all, because his authority accompanies the promotion.

"I will ascend above the tops of the clouds..."

The fourth one, "I will ascend..." is also very similar to the first ascend, if not Heaven, then above the tops of the clouds. This also, is about positioning. Jesus said that the first shall be last and the last shall be first.

> **30But many who are first will be last, and many who are last will be first.**
> **- Matthew 19:30**

Who is Greatest?

> **33 They came to Capernaum. When he was in the house, he asked them, "What were you arguing about on the road?" 34 But they kept quiet because on the way they had argued about who was the greatest.**

³⁵ Sitting down, Jesus called the Twelve and said, "If anyone wants to be first, he must be the very last, and the servant of all."

- Mark 9:33-35.

A Mother's Request

²⁰ Then the mother of Zebedee's sons came to Jesus with her sons and, kneeling down, asked a favor of him.

²¹ "What is it you want?" he asked.
She said, "Grant that one of these two sons of mine may sit at your right and the other at your left in your kingdom."

²² "You don't know what you are asking," Jesus said to them. "Can you drink the cup I am going to drink?"
"We can," they answered.

- Matthew 20:20-22

It is good to desire the best things God has to offer you but disputes about the positions to which the Lord has appointed his people are not pleasing to him. That is why we should not covet the place and positions of others. For we do not know the price they have paid to receive their position. Coveting and jealousy go hand in hand, and this should not be allowed to exist in the house of the Lord.

¹⁵ Such "wisdom" does not come down from heaven but is earthly, unspiritual, of the devil. ¹⁶ For where you have envy and selfish ambition, there you find disorder and every evil practice. ¹⁷ But the wisdom that comes from heaven is first of all pure; then peace-loving, considerate, submissive, full of mercy and good fruit, impartial and sincere.
- James 3:15-17

²⁶ Let us not become conceited, provoking and envying each other. - Galatians 5:26

²¹ For from within, out of men's hearts, come evil thoughts, sexual immorality, theft, murder, adultery, ²² greed, malice, deceit, lewdness, envy, slander, arrogance and folly. ²³ All these evils come from inside and make a man 'unclean.' "
- Mark 7:21-22

These things should not be on the worship platform or in the ones who minister upon the platform. Take a good look at the fruit they bear.

"I will make myself like the Most High..."

The final statement, "I will make myself like the Most High," is the epitome of blasphemy. We can not make ourselves into any-

79

thing, and yet we were created in God's own image. So, as we humble ourselves before his mighty hand, he will form and recreate the image of Christ in us, and we will be true sons and daughters of the Most High. When we allow the Holy Spirit to bring forth the image of Christ already sown in us, we are molded into his very likeness. We are changed from "glory to glory", and his glory is revealed in us.

> [18]But we all, with open face beholding as in a glass the glory of the Lord, are changed into the same image from glory to glory, even as by the Spirit of the Lord.
> - 2 Corinthians 3:18

Pray: There may be some high places of idolatry erected in your worship ministry that may have existed before you arrived. There may have been mistakes by your leadership and things seem to continue to follow a certain pattern, no matter what your intentions are. Josiah was faithful to tear down the high places of idolatry erected long before he became king.

> [8] Josiah brought all the priests from the towns of Judah and desecrated the high places, from Geba to Beersheba, where the priests had burned incense. He broke down the shrines at the gates—at the entrance to

the Gate of Joshua, the city governor, which is on the left of the city gate. [9] Although the priests of the high places did not serve at the altar of the LORD in Jerusalem, they ate unleavened bread with their fellow priests.

- 2 Kings 23:8-9

Lesson: The Holy Spirit may allow you to see what "doors" have been opened or events that may have occurred before your arrival. It is necessary that the land be cleansed, the platform be consecrated before the Lord, and a new path of holiness chartered. As the Lord leads you, he may bring you to a place of repentance on behalf of those who have gone before you, to renounce the mistakes and choices made and to commit to allow the Holy Spirit to lead you from that day forward. And if there are mistakes that you have already made in your ministry, repent and move on to what the Lord has for you. He only wants to bless you with his best, and to remove any stoppages that may hinder his overflowing increase in your life.

Also, if any pride exists simply surrender to his mercy and grace, repent of any pride whether known or not, and allow his humility and his very character to be formed in you. Remember, his character and the fruit of humility formed in you, precedes your promotion in him, if you press on. He is interested in your progress, not your circumventing the process. There are no short cuts around the cross. The shortest route is to pick up your cross and follow him.

Chapter 4
The Holy and the Common

Those Who May Come Near

> ¹⁵ " 'But the priests, who are Levites and descendants of Zadok and who faithfully carried out the duties of my sanctuary when the Israelites went astray from me, are to come near to minister before me; they are to stand before me to offer sacrifices of fat and blood, declares the Sovereign LORD.
>
> ¹⁶ They alone are to enter my sanctuary; they alone are to come near my table to minister before me and perform my service.
> - Ezekiel 44:15-16

The faithful descendents of Zadok were the only ones of the entire Levitical priesthood allowed to come near to his presence and minister unto the Lord, because they did not perform their duties unto the Lord in the presence of idols. All the other Levites did this detestable thing in the sight of the Lord and thus led the people astray, in effect, led them into idolatry.

The priests who were allowed to come near unto the Lord and minister unto him were the ones He commissioned to teach the people the difference between what was Holy and what was common, or profane. It is because the sons of Zadok were faithful to the Lord, that they understood the things which were holy and the things which were profane or called common. Sometimes a common or worldly thing may appear to be good, when it is profane unto the Lord bearing the aroma of idolatry.

> [23] They are to teach my people the difference between the holy and the common and show them how to distinguish between the unclean and the clean. [24] " 'In any dispute, the priests are to serve as judges and decide it according to my ordinances. They are to keep my laws and my decrees for all my appointed feasts, and they are to keep my Sabbaths holy.   - Ezekiel 44:23–24 NIV

> [23] And they shall teach my people the difference between the holy and profane, and cause them to discern between the unclean and the clean. [24] And in controversy they shall stand in judgment; and they shall judge it according to my judgments: and they shall keep my laws and my statutes in all mine assemblies; and they shall hallow my Sabbaths.   - Ezekiel 44:23–24 KJV

This discussion tends to stir up controversy where those who are promoting common practices trying to pass them off as good ideas, raise their heads and say, "How dare you judge me?" or "Who do you think you are to judge me?" According to the Word of God those who are allowed entrance to come near unto the Lord who have a fragrance of his holiness, already have the knowing and understanding of what is holy. They have been granted authority and discernment to know what is holy or pleasing unto the Lord and what is of earthly origin. They are also the ones who will fight even to their detriment to preserve and protect that which is holy, as well as those things that maintain that level of glory and holiness. They have become accustomed to his glory and his goodness, and can't live without it.

Once they have tasted his glory, his holiness, and his presence, they cannot live outside of the precious fragrance it bestows upon their lives. So this may appear to be judgmental, when they are really preserving the very lifeblood of what they have become, "Holy unto the Lord." The glory and the holiness of the Lord bring accountability, of which many resist. This is due to the change and fear of losing control or fear of the unknown. Yet the priests, who have come into this place of understanding and right standing with the Lord, are still beckoned to follow him.

And so, you say, "What is Holy and what is profane?" The Lord has shown me several examples and the consequences of the choices made, through his Word. Let's look at Moses.

Did you ever wonder what led the people to make the golden calf anyway, which was the first place idolatry was performed after the Israelites deliverance from Egypt? It is found in the first verse of Exodus 32

The Golden Calf

[1] When the people saw that Moses was so long in coming down from the mountain, they gathered around Aaron and said, "Come, make us gods who will go before us. <u>As for this fellow Moses who brought us up out of Egypt, we don't know what has happened to him.</u>"

[2] Aaron answered them, "Take off the gold earrings that your wives, your sons and your daughters are wearing, and bring them to me." [3] So all the people took off their earrings and brought them to Aaron.

- Exodus 32:1-3

Their first mistake was to attempt to bring Moses down to a lower, common standing with them. Here is the anointed, appointed deliverer who just demonstrated 10 plagues upon the Egyptians, and delivered them through the Red Sea witnessing their enemies' annihilation. This is what they said of Moses, they called him "this fellow Moses." Now when I think of a "fellow", I think of one right alongside me, of the same standing, or going bowling with the "fellows." They did not recognize or speak about him with reverence as the man of God, not that they were to put him on a pedestal or a platform. He was the one called by God to meet with him face to face, to hear and receive the very words of God, and to deliver the judgments of God. Have a little more respect! I believe this was the first step into idolatry, they did what was right in their own eyes, and missed it, big time!

Lesson: The lesson here is to know those among you who are "Holy unto the Lord." They are the Lord's, they are called for his service, and they are called to lead his people. It's like E. F. Hutton, as the commercial says, "When E. F. Hutton speaks, people listen." These people have been trained on the backside of the wilderness in the things of God, and their training is to impart the wisdom and lessons of God to those who don't have to live in the wilderness for 40 years! If you honor the people of God and receive freely what their blood, sweat, and tears have given you, you will not "accidentally" step into a place of idolatry, or into sin with consequences you can't possibly see on the other side of your choice. When they speak, I would listen, it might save you a lot of heartache. Here's another excerpt from Moses' life.

Miriam and Aaron Oppose Moses

1 Miriam and Aaron began to talk against Moses because of his Cushite wife, for he had married a Cushite. 2 "Has the LORD spoken only through Moses?" they asked. "Hasn't he also spoken through us?" And the LORD heard this.

3 (Now Moses was a very humble man, more humble than anyone else on the face of the earth.)*

4 At once the LORD said to Moses, Aaron and Miriam, "Come out to the Tent of Meeting, all three of you." So the three of them came out. 5 Then the LORD came down in a pillar of cloud; he stood at the entrance to the Tent and summoned Aaron and Miriam.

When both of them stepped forward, [6] he said, "Listen to my words:
"When a prophet of the LORD is among you,
I reveal myself to him in visions,
I speak to him in dreams.
[7] But this is not true of my servant Moses;
he is faithful in all my house.
[8] With him I speak face to face,
clearly and not in riddles;
he sees the form of the LORD.
Why then were you not afraid
to speak against my servant Moses?"

[9] The anger of the LORD burned against them, and he left them.

[10] When the cloud lifted from above the Tent, there stood Miriam — leprous, like snow. Aaron turned toward her and saw that she had leprosy; [11] and he said to Moses, "Please, my lord, do not hold against us the sin we have so foolishly committed. [12] Do not let her be like a stillborn infant coming from its mother's womb with its flesh half eaten away."

[13] So Moses cried out to the LORD, "O God, please heal her!"

[14] The LORD replied to Moses, "If her father had spit in her face, would she not have been in disgrace for seven days? Confine her outside the camp for seven days; after that

she can be brought back." [15] So Miriam was confined outside the camp for seven days, and the people did not move on till she was brought back.   - Numbers 12:1-14

Lesson: The second lesson that we learn here is a parallel to the operation of the anointing. When some experience the anointing under their leader, they may think they can function as well as their leader out on their own. They have already taken the first steps toward rebellion. As one is called by God, promoted into that place of leadership by God, many times the anointing and the fragrance of what is on their life trickles down to the members of the team. When working with different people you will find that each has their own style or flow that greatly affects the way you and your team operate on the worship platform. It is because you are operating under that person's mantle of authority. This is also true of your worship leader. When grumblings and complaints about the leader arise, jealousy of their place and position is usually the root. Complaining, grumbling people wandered in the wilderness and never saw their Promised Land. Look at the end of verse 8, it says, "**Why then were** you not afraid to speak against my servant Moses?" The Lord is speaking of the fear of the Lord for their rebellion against the Lord, even though it was directed at Moses. This attribute of the "fear of the Lord" will again come back into the church.

As you see, God always stood behind his man of authority, and Miriam paid for her rebellion and seeming "equality" with the man of God. This resulted in her being stricken with leprosy, which caused her to be thrown out of the camp for 7 days. Incidentally, in God's mercy, he spared Aaron, the High Priest from getting leprosy, or he would have tainted the entire Levitical priesthood, because Aaron would have been deemed unclean and unfit for service. The people saw this entire scene take place and still there was another rebellion brewing against the man of God. We have already visited this example in scripture, concerning Korah's Rebellion in Numbers 16. They took Moses down a notch and elevated themselves, and they gathered their numbers and stood in the majority to oppose Moses. You would think that they had seen enough of God's glory and his power demonstrated in front of them. They had hardened their hearts, and of course pride was at the root of their insurrection, as well as rebellion.

These leaders God has placed over our lives may be saving us from things we cannot see that might cause lengthy detours in our path with God. I have spent a lot of time and effort to bring this issue to light. This issue is prevalent in many other ministries outside of worship. But in the last day army, the Army of the Lord will advance, staying within rank and position, no one thrusting another with his own sword. This is what the Lord's Army looks like in Joel 2.

> **7 They shall run like mighty men; they shall climb the wall like men of war; and they shall march every one on his ways, and they shall not break their ranks:**
>
> **8 Neither shall one thrust another; they shall walk every one in his path: and when they fall upon the sword, they shall not be wounded.   - Joel 2:7-8 KJV**

Let's look at a New Testament perspective from the early church in Acts 5.

Ananias and Sapphira

1 Now a man named Ananias, together with his wife Sapphira, also sold a piece of property. 2 With his wife's full knowledge he kept back part of the money for himself, but brought the rest and put it at the apostles' feet.

3 Then Peter said, "Ananias, how is it that Satan has so filled your heart that you have lied to the Holy Spirit and have kept for yourself some of the money you received for the land? 4 Didn't it belong to you before it was sold? And after it was sold, wasn't the money at your disposal? What made you think of doing such a thing? You have not lied to men but to God."

5 When Ananias heard this, he fell down and died. And great fear seized all who heard what had happened. 6 Then the young men came forward, wrapped up his body, and carried him out and buried him. 7 About three hours later his wife came in, not knowing what had happened. 8 Peter asked her, "Tell me, is this the price you and Ananias got for the land?" "Yes," she said, "that is the price."

9 Peter said to her, "How could you agree to test the Spirit of the Lord? Look! The feet of the men who buried your husband are at the door, and they will carry you out also." 10 At

that moment she fell down at his feet and died. Then the young men came in and, finding her dead, carried her out and buried her beside her husband. [11] <u>Great fear seized the whole church and all who heard about these events.</u>   - Acts 5:1-11

Notice the difference between the Israelites reaction to what they witnessed of the Lord's judgment, and the next verse after what the early church witnessed.

[41] <u>The next day the whole Israelite community grumbled against Moses and Aaron. "You have killed the LORD's people," they said</u>.   - Numbers 16:41

[10] <u>At that moment she fell down at his feet and died. Then the young men came in and, finding her dead, carried her out and buried her beside her husband. [11] Great fear seized the whole church and all who heard about these events</u>.   - Acts 5:10-11

The Fruit of Correction

[12] The apostles performed many miraculous signs and wonders among the people. And all the believers used to meet together in Solomon's Colonnade. [13] No one else dared join them, even though they were highly re-

garded by the people. [14] Nevertheless, more and more men and women believed in the Lord and were added to their number.

[15] As a result, people brought the sick into the streets and laid them on beds and mats so that at least Peter's shadow might fall on some of them as he passed by. [16] Crowds gathered also from the towns around Jerusalem, bringing their sick and those tormented by evil spirits, and all of them were healed.
- Acts 5:12-16

This awesome display resulted in a fear of the Lord and a reverence for the things of God including the leaders God appointed. There was no grumbling or gossip or backbiting or rioting. There was only respect. Some things should be left untouched by man, because those things belong to the Lord. God has a way of dealing with his people, either in correction because he loves them, or in judgment because they will not bend or return unto the Lord. This segment deals with the people or leaders God has appointed. I believe each one of these examples demonstrates God's judgment for rebellion or covetousness. Also, for the New Testament believer, it can disqualify us from fulfilling our calling. I believe God will use us in every capacity he can. These are character tests. If we fail these tests, we cannot be entrusted with what God is calling us to do. I believe we need to build and honor a man in his field, and when we have matured, God will then give us our own field. Where is God's heart in all of this? Can he trust us to not hurt his little ones? Can he trust us to lead them in his holy and righteous ways, or will we lead them to follow us in our own agendas and ambitions?

Who were the Kohathites?

For the entire context concerning the function of the Kohathites read Numbers 4:1-20. They were a particular branch of the Levites chosen by the Lord to take care of the holy furnishings of the "Tent of Meeting." They were in charge of wrapping all the furnishings in cloths for transporting the Tent of Meeting. I have included a few of these instructions which were specific to their responsibilities.

> ⁴ "This is the work of the Kohathites in the Tent of Meeting: the care of the <u>most holy things</u>. ⁵ When the camp is to move, Aaron and his sons are to go in and take down the shielding curtain and cover the ark of the Testimony with it.
>
> ¹⁵ "After Aaron and his sons have finished covering the <u>holy furnishings and all the</u>

holy articles, and when the camp is ready to move, the Kohathites are to come to do the carrying. But they must not touch the holy things or they will die. The Kohathites are to carry those things that are in the Tent of Meeting.

He is to be in charge of the entire tabernacle and everything in it, including its holy furnishings and articles."

17 The LORD said to Moses and Aaron, 18 "See that the Kohathite tribal clans are not cut off from the Levites. 19 So that they may live and not die when they come near the most holy things, do this for them: Aaron and his sons are to go into the sanctuary and assign to each man his work and what he is to carry. 20 But the Kohathites must not go in to look at the holy things, even for a moment, or they will die."
- Numbers 4:4-5, 15-20

God has regard for his holy things. They are blessed of him, symbolic of things to come, and I believe they retain the anointing of God. The ark was considered so holy man was not to touch it and those who did, died. It says the Lord's anger burned against them.

The Ark Brought to Jerusalem

¹ David again brought together out of Israel chosen men, thirty thousand in all. ² He and all his men set out from Baalah of Judah to bring up from there the ark of God, which is called by the Name, the name of the LORD Almighty, who is enthroned between the cherubim that are on the ark. ³ They set the ark of God on a new cart and brought it from the house of Abinadab, which was on the hill. Uzzah and Ahio, sons of Abinadab, were guiding the new cart ⁴ with the ark of God on it, and Ahio was walking in front of it. ⁵ David and the whole house of Israel were celebrating with all their might before the LORD, with songs and with harps, lyres, tambourines, sistrums and cymbals.

⁶ When they came to the threshing floor of Nacon, Uzzah reached out and took hold of the ark of God, because the oxen stumbled. ⁷The LORD's anger burned against Uzzah because of his irreverent act; therefore God struck him down and he died there beside the ark of God.   - 2 Samuel 6:1-7

In verse 7 the Lord calls Uzzah's act, "irreverent." As we go higher in God, respect for the things of God is crucial. I believe this to be symbolic of touching the anointed things of God with the arm of flesh which represents all that is unclean. The ark can symbolize those vessels that carry his presence or his glory which actually refers to his people. The holy things of God can symbolize a ministry or the worship itself. Anything of pure origin that man tries to get his hands on, change its direction, or cause it to adhere to an agenda, is touching the holy things of God. What about when we try to force the Holy Spirit to tag along with us in the direction of our choosing, instead of letting him lead us in the direction God intends for us to go? If we are not careful, we can stifle the Holy Spirit's ability to move through us and through the use of manipulation and control force him out of our churches. Man's control and stipulation of what the Holy Spirit is allowed to do or how he is allowed to move grieves the Lord. We must be cautious when trying to direct a move of God, or we will show it the door.

In regards to worship, let us revisit the original text.

10 The Levites who went far from me when Israel went astray and who wandered from me after their idols must bear the consequences of their sin. 11 They may serve in my sanctuary, having charge of the gates of the temple and serving in it; they may slaughter

the burnt offerings and sacrifices for the people and stand before the people and serve them.

[12] But because they served them in the presence of their idols and made the house of Israel fall into sin, therefore I have sworn with uplifted hand that they must bear the consequences of their sin, declares the Sovereign LORD. [13] They are not to come near to serve me as priests or come near any of my holy things or my most holy offerings; they must bear the shame of their detestable practices. [14] Yet I will put them in charge of the duties of the temple and all the work that is to be done in it.

[15] " 'But the priests, who are Levites and descendants of Zadok and who faithfully carried out the duties of my sanctuary when the Israelites went astray from me, are to come near to minister before me; they are to stand before me to offer sacrifices of fat and blood, declares the Sovereign LORD. [16] They alone are to enter my sanctuary; they alone are to come near my table to minister before me and perform my service.- Ezekiel 44:10-16

The Levites were allowed to serve the people, serve in the church, stand before the people to serve them, and handle the basic workings of the sanctuary. However, they brought in common and profane things into the sanctuary and actually through it introduced idolatry into the house of the Lord and to the people as well. They probably seemed like good things to do, similar to good programs which program the Holy Spirit right out of his place in the church. Sometimes worship can be fun, everyone jumping around, with high volume and high intensity. It sounds much like the world, and even has the appearance of American Idol. It may sound good, look good, and be flashy, resulting in a great performance. But that's where it stops; there is no presence, no power, no anointing, and no Holy Spirit. It resembles so much of the world, it looks like the world, sounds like the world, it is the world. The fruit doesn't fall far from the tree.

Stealing the limelight = Stealing the glory for yourself

Performance = Idolatry

It is common or worldly and it has invaded platforms all across the church landscape of America, and no one pointed out that it is common, and thus profane unto the Lord. In some churches, they worship "the worship." This is idolatry in the very face of the One who is supposed to be worshipped. Worshipping a ministry or a particular anointing or a person is still idolatry, and we find some of these high places that have been erected in the church will have to be torn down, as in Josiah's day. Does this remind you of the golden calf?

> ² Aaron answered them, "Take off the gold earrings that your wives, your sons and your daughters are wearing, and bring them to me." ³ So all the people took off their earrings and brought them to Aaron. ⁴ <u>He took what they handed him and made it into an idol cast in the shape of a calf, fashioning it with a tool. Then they said, "These are your gods, O Israel, who brought you up out of Egypt."</u>
>
> ⁵ <u>When Aaron saw this, he built an altar in front of the calf and announced, "Tomorrow there will be a festival to the LORD."</u> ⁶ So the next day the people rose early and sacrificed burnt offerings and presented fellowship offerings. Afterward they sat down to eat and drink and got up to indulge in revelry.　　　　　- Exodus 32:2-6

God may have to throw the golden calf into the fire!

When the Glory departed

There are two times the Glory departed from the Temple. The first was recorded in Ezekiel chapter 10.

The Glory Departs From the Temple

[1] I looked, and I saw the likeness of a throne of sapphire above the expanse that was over the heads of the cherubim. [2] The LORD said to the man clothed in linen, "Go in among the wheels beneath the cherubim. Fill your hands with burning coals from among the cherubim and scatter them over the city." And as I watched, he went in.

[3] Now the cherubim were standing on the south side of the temple when the man went in, and a cloud filled the inner court. [4] Then the glory of the LORD rose from above the cherubim and moved to the threshold of the temple. The cloud filled the temple, and the court was full of the radiance of the glory of the LORD. [5] The sound of the wings of the cherubim could be heard as far away as the outer court, like the voice of God Almighty when he speaks.

[18] Then the glory of the LORD departed from over the threshold of the temple and stopped above the cherubim. [19] While I watched, the cherubim spread their wings

and rose from the ground, and as they went, the wheels went with them. They stopped at the entrance to the east gate of the LORD's house, and the glory of the God of Israel was above them.   - Ezekiel 10:1-5, 18-19

[18] "They will return to it and remove all its vile images and detestable idols. [19] I will give them an undivided heart and put a new spirit in them; I will remove from them their heart of stone and give them a heart of flesh. [20] Then they will follow my decrees and be careful to keep my laws. They will be my people, and I will be their God. [21] But as for those whose hearts are devoted to their vile images and detestable idols, I will bring down on their own heads what they have done, declares the Sovereign LORD."

[22] Then the cherubim, with the wheels beside them, spread their wings, and the glory of the God of Israel was above them. [23] The glory of the LORD went up from within the city and stopped above the mountain east of it. [24] The Spirit lifted me up and brought me to the exiles in Babylonia in the vision given by the Spirit of God. Ezekiel 11:18-24

Did you notice in verses 4, 18 and 19, it says that the Glory moved to the threshold, stopped at the threshold, and stopped again at the east gate? It is as if the Glory was looking back at his dwelling place, his residence, his home, not wanting to leave it behind, but had to keep moving forward. What compelled the glory to leave its dwelling place? It was the mixture of the Holy and the profane in the temple. Idolatry had infiltrated the temple, and the Glory which is holy, could not remain, because it could not be in the same place with such vile wickedness. The Glory departed from the east gate, but will once again return through the east gate to take up his residence.

The Glory departs a second time

The second time I believe the Glory departed was in the early 300s AD when Emperor Constantine eradicated the persecution of Christians, and thus dictated tolerance for the Christians. This was a huge sigh of relief for the Christians who had endured extreme forms of persecution; however his efforts did not reach far enough. He declared that Christianity would be the official religion of the state for political reasons, yet he did not renounce or forbid the pagan cults of the time. In fact many of the pagan temples now incorporated their idolatrous practices into their new found state formed religion, Christianity. Many idolatrous practices were not forbidden, and even allowed, including the worship of the sun god, which many Christians of that day observed. Thus the Holy and the common were intermixed. I believe with this mixture, the lights went out in the Church and thrust the Church into the dark ages. Idolatry was tolerated and accepted hand in hand with Christianity.

The second day ministry was birthed and we have endured 1700 years of this ministry, one diluted by idolatry, and a form of "godliness, but denying the power." In both examples, idolatry introduced into the house of the Lord caused the Glory to leave the church, and the lights to go out! Yet God has had a single candle here and there burning brightly all throughout the ages, the light was never allowed to go out. Can you see the scheme of the devil? If he could not wipe out Christianity with killing the believers of it, he would dilute its power by mixing idolatry with Christianity in the church. Thus his kingdom would not be shaken and he could not be unseated, because of a powerless gospel operating without the Glory. During this time, the church prospered, built magnificent monuments of cathedrals, and spread with riches and fame. Who was the rewarder of the church, and the prosperer of it? The devil will allow you to have a little anointing and reward with great riches, as long as you have little power and authority, with no real threat to overthrow his kingdom. Even today the devil still offers this temptation to those who dare to remain pure, their ministries as well as themselves, as exemplified in the third temptation of Jesus in the wilderness, of which we have already discussed.

And I see America in this. We have allowed Christianity to function side by side with the toleration of other pagan religions. We have reduced our God to only deity in common standing with other gods, as equals. If we are not careful to stand up and take back our nation as a "nation under GOD," we might see our lights go out as well, and the Glory leave our churches and our nation. This is a serious offense to our Lord, enough so as to be the only record of when and why the Glory left the temple. The third time will be when the abomination takes up residence in the temple again, during the half marker of the tribulation. It will be devastating.

The last example of that which is holy pertains to the very presence and attributes of God.

8 "I am the LORD; that is my name!
I will not give my glory to another
or my praise to idols.   - Isaiah 42:8

11 For my own sake, for my own sake, I do
this. How can I let myself be defamed?
I will not yield my glory to another.
                                      - Isaiah 48:11

Some things belong to the Lord. The Glory is one of them. He will bestow his Glory upon those who will not skim a portion off for themselves. These are tried and trustworthy servants who will not touch it for themselves. Moses was called one of the most humble men who ever lived, and thus the one who saw his Glory as the Lord passed by, speaking with God face to face. One of the prerequisites for this kind of Glory is humility which is usually brought forth through suffering. Phil. 2:3-11

16 The Spirit himself testifies with our spirit that we are God's children. 17 Now if we are children, then we are heirs—heirs of God and co-heirs with Christ, <u>if indeed we share in his sufferings in order that we may also share in his glory.</u> 18 <u>I consider that our present sufferings are not worth comparing with the glory that will be revealed in us</u>.
                                      - Romans 8:16-18

Sometimes the only path to become qualified to carry his Glory is the path of humility, sharing in the fellowship of Christ's sufferings. Only then will we be able to carry his Glory without allowing our arm of flesh to touch it, or the soul to control it. God will only give this to those whose character has been tested through trial and much affliction, in other words to take up our cross and follow him. He had to go to the cross, and so must we. The path to the glory must go through the cross; there is no detour or sidestepping the cross.

What does this man look like?

2 Consider it pure joy, my brothers, whenever you face trials of many kinds, 3 because you know that the testing of your faith develops perseverance. 4 Perseverance must finish its work so that you may be mature and complete, not lacking anything. 5 If any of you lacks wisdom, he should ask God, who gives generously to all without finding fault, and it will be given to him.

6 But when he asks, he must believe and not doubt, because he who doubts is like a wave of the sea, blown and tossed by the wind. 7 That man should not think he will receive anything from the Lord; 8 he is a double-minded man, unstable in all he does.

⁹ The brother in humble circumstances ought to take pride in his high position.

- James 1:2-9

This is the one God will entrust with his glory. And we see in this passage that God has thoroughly tested this man's character, resulting in maturity and completeness, having a faith that doesn't get tossed back and forth with every wave of every storm. Someone once said, "If you haven't been through something, you don't have anything to say!" Look at how the Lord honors the one who is humble, he says he is in a high position, and that is only the Lord's to give.

Chapter 5
Crossing the Jordan River

The Priests go first

Let us look at a familiar passage of scripture as pertaining to worship.

> ¹ Early in the morning Joshua and all the Israelites set out from Shittim and went to the Jordan, where they camped before crossing over. ² After three days the officers went throughout the camp, ³ giving orders to the people: "When you see the ark of the covenant of the LORD your God, and the priests, who are Levites, carrying it, you are to move out from your positions and follow it. ⁴ Then you will know which way to go, since you have never been this way before. But keep a distance of about a thousand yards between you and the ark; do not go near it."
>
> ⁵ Joshua told the people, "Consecrate yourselves, for tomorrow the LORD will do amazing things among you."

⁶ Joshua said to the priests, "Take up the ark of the covenant and pass on ahead of the people." So they took it up and went ahead of them.

⁷ And the LORD said to Joshua, "Today I will begin to exalt you in the eyes of all Israel, so they may know that I am with you as I was with Moses. ⁸ Tell the priests who carry the ark of the covenant: 'When you reach the edge of the Jordan's waters, go and stand in the river.' "

⁹ Joshua said to the Israelites, "Come here and listen to the words of the LORD your God. ¹⁰ This is how you will know that the living God is among you and that he will certainly drive out before you the Canaanites, Hittites, Hivites, Perizzites, Girgashites, Amorites and Jebusites. ¹¹ See, the ark of the covenant of the Lord of all the earth will go into the Jordan ahead of you. ¹² Now then, choose twelve men from the tribes of Israel, one from each tribe. ¹³ And as soon as the priests who carry the ark of the LORD -the Lord of all the earth—set foot in the Jordan, its waters flowing downstream will be cut off and stand up in a heap."

¹⁴ So when the people broke camp to cross the Jordan, the priests carrying the ark of the covenant went ahead of them. ¹⁵ Now the Jordan is at flood stage all during harvest.

Yet as soon as the priests who carried the ark reached the Jordan and their feet touched the water's edge, [16] the water from upstream stopped flowing. It piled up in a heap a great distance away, at a town called Adam in the vicinity of Zarethan, while the water flowing down to the Sea of the Arabah was completely cut off. So the people crossed over opposite Jericho. [17] The priests who carried the ark of the covenant of the LORD stood firm on dry ground in the middle of the Jordan, while all Israel passed by until the whole nation had completed the crossing on dry ground.

- Joshua 3:1-17

[10] Now the priests who carried the ark remained standing in the middle of the Jordan until everything the LORD had commanded Joshua was done by the people, just as Moses had directed Joshua. The people hurried over, [11] and as soon as all of them had crossed, the ark of the LORD and the priests came to the other side while the people watched.

- Joshua 4:10-11

What does this have to do with worship? It is usually referring to crossing over to the Promised Land; the old generation had all passed away and the new generation was empowered to finally make this long awaited journey. We already talked about the priesthood that was called to carry the ark. They were the only ones allowed to even touch it, and yet they had to use long poles to transport the ark. But I believe this picture represents what we do as worshippers and as priests of the Lord. It is interesting that in verse 3, he gives the orders to the people that when they see the ark carried by the priests; they are to move out from their positions and follow it. Look at verse 4, "**⁴ Then you will know which way to go, since you have never been this way before.**"

The priests were led by the Lord "...in the way they were to go..." and the people were to follow. To me this resembles a worship service where the Holy Ghost is free to lead the worshippers, and the direction becomes clear as the flow of the service unfolds and his purposes are revealed. The priests had been given very clear instruction, though not the entire plan, only the next few steps ahead. Also notice in verse 5 that Joshua instructed the people to be consecrated for the awesome things God was about to do. The people had a part in the preparation as well. Their hearts were to be ready to receive what the Lord had in store for them.

⁶ Joshua said to the priests, "Take up the ark of the covenant and pass on ahead of the

<u>people."</u> So they took it up and went ahead of them.

⁸ <u>Tell the priests who carry the ark of the</u> <u>covenant: 'When you reach the edge of the</u> <u>Jordan's waters, go and stand in the river.'</u>
- Joshua 3: 6 and 8

The priests were instructed to go ahead of the people and to literally step into the middle of the river and stand. First of all, the priests were deemed qualified to carry the Lord's presence. We as worshippers, like the priests, are called to carry his presence, the very essence of the Glory of God in our lives which spills out into our ministry unto the Lord.

Lesson: Incidentally, I sometimes refer to "the ark" as "the ark of his presence", which parallels our function as priests that carry the Glory of his presence today. The ark symbolized his presence going with them, and the enemies of this nation would literally see the ark go before them and begin to tremble in fear. They knew the God of Israel was with them, and this ark, the presence of the Almighty God set them apart from all other nations. This is the example of how we are set apart by the Glory of the presence of God. The fol-

115

lowing verses give the scriptural reference of how this should parallel our priesthood today.

14 The LORD replied, "My Presence will go with you, and I will give you rest."
15 Then Moses said to him, "If your Presence does not go with us, do not send us up from here. - Exodus 33:14-15

Joshua 3:17 and Joshua 4:10-11 record what the priests actually did, they stood:

17 The priests who carried the ark of the covenant of the LORD stood firm on dry ground in the middle of the Jordan, while all Israel passed by until the whole nation had completed the crossing on dry ground. - Joshua 3:17

10 Now the priests who carried the ark remained standing in the middle of the Jordan until everything the LORD had commanded Joshua was done by the people, just as Moses had directed Joshua. The people hurried over, 11 and as soon as all of them had crossed, the ark of the LORD and the priests came to the other side while the people watched. - Joshua 4:10-11

116

The priests who were carrying the ark of his presence walked into the river and literally stood the ground until all the people had crossed over on dry ground. Take a look at the Jordan River:

> [15] <u>Now the Jordan is at flood stage all during harvest. Yet as soon as the priests who carried the ark reached the Jordan and their feet touched the water's edge,</u> [16] <u>the water from upstream stopped flowing. It piled up in a heap a great distance away, at a town called Adam in the vicinity of Zarethan, while the water flowing down to the Sea of the Arabah (the Salt Sea) was completely cut off.</u>   - Joshua 3:15-16

There may have been some apprehension walking into a river that was at flood stage. That's why their "feat" was so magnificent and truly a miracle. The river was at flood stage because of the season of the harvest. We are currently in this "season of the harvest". The river may be high and raging and seemingly impossible to cross, but it is for the purpose of the harvest that the miracle and the Glory of God are demonstrated. Not until every person safely crossed the river did the priests then continue to the other side.

Now watch this. The priests go on before the people through worship, and they come to that prophetic flow represented by the Jordan River. The Holy Spirit gently leads them through to stand the ground as the purposes of God are revealed. It is in this flow that the purposes and directions of God are revealed "since they have never gone that way before." When all is accomplished, the Holy Spirit then gently leads the priests or worshippers, safely to the other side.

I believe this to be a picture of the worshipping priests who carry the glory and stand their ground until the entire church has crossed over into the Glory.

This is what prophetic worship looks like. Understand, this kind of ministry requires the priests to be prepared and taught how to follow the Holy Spirit's lead. They must learn how to wade into the river, in sync and unity of purpose. They must be consecrated and trained in how to carry the Glory of God's presence.

There are several passages where the worshippers went ahead of the armies of the Lord as in Psalm 68.

²⁴ Your procession has come into view, O God, the procession of my God and King into the sanctuary.

²⁵ In front are the singers, after them the musicians; with them are the maidens playing tambourines.

²⁶ Praise God in the great congregation; praise the LORD in the assembly of Israel.
                              - Psalm 68:24-26

The praisers and the worshippers were historically positioned in front of the armies of the Lord. Let us look at the first occurrence noted in scripture.

¹³ They set out, this first time, at the LORD's command through Moses. ¹⁴ <u>The divisions of the camp of Judah went first, under their standard.</u> Nahshon son of Amminadab was in command.   - Numbers 10:13-14

Judah went first. What was the significance of Judah going first? Let's go back a little further.

³⁵ She conceived again, and when she gave birth to a son she said, "This time I will praise the LORD." So she named him Judah. Then she stopped having children.
                              - Genesis 29:35

The name Judah means "praise" or "thanks." Judah was the tribe that King David and his royal line came from and ultimately King Jesus.

> ⁵ **When a trumpet blast is sounded, the tribes camping on the east are to set out.**
> - **Numbers 10:5**

What is significant is that Judah led the tribes out from the east. In Ezekiel the east gate signifies the way of the return of the Glory of the Lord and the King of Kings will return through this east gate. We will cover this more in depth in the next chapter. There is one more example of the strategy of prophetic worship.

Many of us are familiar with the story of Jehoshaphat, which powerfully illustrates the strategies of God coming through the prophetic word and powerful praise in the midst of surrounding armies.

> ¹⁴ **Then the Spirit of the LORD came upon Jahaziel son of Zechariah, the son of Benaiah, the son of Jeiel, the son of Mattaniah, a Levite and descendant of Asaph, as he stood in the assembly.**
>
> ¹⁵ **He said: "Listen, King Jehoshaphat and all who live in Judah and Jerusalem! This is**

what the LORD says to you: 'Do not be afraid or discouraged because of this vast army. <u>For the battle is not yours, but God's.</u> ¹⁶ Tomorrow march down against them. They will be climbing up by the Pass of Ziz, and you will find them at the end of the gorge in the Desert of Jeruel.

¹⁷ You will not have to fight this battle. <u>Take up your positions; stand firm and see the deliverance the LORD will give you, O Judah</u> and Jerusalem. Do not be afraid; do not be discouraged. <u>Go out to face them tomorrow, and the LORD will be with you.</u>' "

¹⁸ <u>Jehoshaphat bowed with his face to the ground, and all the people of Judah and Jerusalem fell down in worship before the LORD.</u> ¹⁹ <u>Then some Levites from the Kohathites and Korahites stood up and praised the LORD, the God of Israel, with very loud voice.</u>

²⁰ Early in the morning they left for the Desert of Tekoa. As they set out, Jehoshaphat stood and said, "Listen to me, Judah and people of Jerusalem! Have faith in the LORD your God and you will be upheld; have faith in his prophets and you will be successful."
²¹ <u>After consulting the people, Jehoshaphat appointed men to sing to the LORD and to praise him for the splendor of his holiness as they went out at the head of the army,</u>

saying: "Give thanks to the LORD,
for his love endures forever."

²² As they began to sing and praise, the
LORD set ambushes against the men of Ammon and Moab and Mount Seir who were in-
vading Judah, and they were defeated. ²³ The
men of Ammon and Moab rose up against
the men from Mount Seir to destroy and an-
nihilate them. After they finished slaughter-
ing the men from Seir, they helped to destroy one another.

²⁴ When the men of Judah came to the place
that overlooks the desert and looked toward
the vast army, they saw only dead bodies lying on the ground; no one had escaped.

- 2 Chronicles 20:14-24

Notice in verse 14, a Levite and descen-
dant of Asaph (King David's chief seer or
prophet, who was appointed over those who
prophesied with cymbals), received the strategy
of the Lord and boldly declared it and encouraged the King and his people. He said that the
battle was the Lord's and not theirs to fight. I
believe when we praise and war through worship, we are entering the strategy and battle
plans of the Lord, we are not fighting it in our
own strength, but are employing the game plan
and the perfect strategy that will bring the
Lord's victory.

In verse 17, he says to take up your positions, stand firm and see the deliverance of the Lord. Does this sound familiar? Are you reminded of the priests that stood the ground while the people crossed over to take possession of their land? He even told them to go out and face their enemy, for the Lord was with them. Isn't it like the Lord to show us how to stand our ground praising him, not to escape the confrontation, but to face the enemy with the weaponry of worship, looking upon the literal destruction of our enemies and the deliverance that came from his mighty hand? Our God doesn't want us to just know that he gave us the victory. He wants us to see it with our own eyes and know that we are a participant with him in the victory, through employing our powerful weaponry of worship. He wants to boost our faith and our belief in his faithfulness and goodness to us by experiencing the victory.

In verse 22 shows what was accomplished by their praise. While they were singing of his enduring love and faithfulness to them, declaring his holiness in the face of the enemy, the Lord himself set up ambushes and defeated the enemy in the very same moments their praises were going up. There was no time delay in the action of the Lord, it was a done deal. The only delay was when they actually saw what had been done, but it was settled as their praises reached Heaven. I think also that their declaration of the holiness of their God in the face of the enemy was significantly powerful and wielded a lethal blow to the enemy. I am reminded once again of how our King wars against the enemy:

The Rider on the White Horse

> [11] I saw heaven standing open and there before me was a white horse, whose rider is called Faithful and True. With justice he judges and makes war. [12] His eyes are like blazing fire, and on his head are many crowns. He has a name written on him that no one knows but he himself. [13] He is dressed in a robe dipped in blood, and his name is the Word of God. [14] <u>The armies of heaven were following him, riding on white horses and dressed in fine linen, white and clean. [15] Out of his mouth comes a sharp sword with which to strike down the nations</u>. "He will rule them with an iron scepter." He treads the winepress of the fury of the wrath of God Almighty. [16] On his robe and on his thigh he has this name written: KING OF KINGS AND LORD OF LORDS.
>
> - Revelation 19:11-16

Chapter 6
The Key of David

Lesson from another worship leader

> 7 "To the angel of the church in Philadelphia
> write:
> These are the words of him who is holy and
> true, who holds the key of David. What he
> opens no one can shut, and what he shuts no
> one can open.   - Revelation 3:7

I believe we can glean some important truths
from another worship leader, David, the sweet
psalmist of Israel. There is testimony from God
himself concerning this worshipper. Let's see
what the Lord has to record about him.

The Genealogy of David

> 13 So Boaz took Ruth and she became his
> wife. Then he went to her, and the LORD
> enabled her to conceive, and she gave birth
> to a son. 14 The women said to Naomi:
> "Praise be to the LORD, who this day has

not left you without a kinsman-redeemer. May he become famous throughout Israel! [15] He will renew your life and sustain you in your old age. For your daughter-in-law, who loves you and who is better to you than seven sons, has given him birth."

[16] Then Naomi took the child, laid him in her lap and cared for him. [17] The women living there said, "Naomi has a son." And they named him Obed. He was the father of Jesse, the father of David.   - Ruth 4:13-16

How fitting that the Word of God should record David's lineage. He was the grandson of Ruth and Boaz, her kinsman redeemer, a picture of who Jesus is to us. Messianic Prophecy was already a part of his lineage, and Ruth was faithful and lay at the feet of Boaz. Boaz declared, "[12] Although it is true that I am near of kin, there is a kinsman-redeemer nearer than I." (Ruth 3:12)

Could it be that David's heart for worship, to "lay at the feet of his God," came from his grandmother and the Messianic prophetic declarations from his grandfather?

Let's look at David's heart for worship in his own words.

[8] I love the house where you live, O LORD,
the place where your glory dwells.
- Psalm 26:8

[4] One thing I ask of the LORD,
this is what I seek:
that I may dwell in the house of the
LORD
all the days of my life,
to gaze upon the beauty of the LORD
and to seek him in his temple.
- Psalm 27:4

[7] The LORD is my strength and my shield;
my heart trusts in him, and I am helped.
My heart leaps for joy
and I will give thanks to him in song.
- Psalm 28:7

[1] The LORD is my shepherd, I shall not be in
want.
[2] He makes me lie down in green pastures,
he leads me beside quiet waters,
[3] he restores my soul.
He guides me in paths of righteousness
for his name's sake.
[4] Even though I walk
through the valley of the shadow of
death,
I will fear no evil,
for you are with me;
your rod and your staff,
they comfort me.

⁵ You prepare a table before me
in the presence of my enemies.
You anoint my head with oil;
my cup overflows.
⁶ Surely goodness and love will follow me
all the days of my life, and I will dwell in
the house of the LORD forever.

- Psalm 23:1-6

¹⁴ May the words of my mouth and the meditation of my heart be pleasing in your sight,
O LORD, my Rock and my Redeemer.

- Psalm 19:14

After reading just a few of the words that
came from David's heart, can you feel the love
that melted his heart when he thought of David?
This is the Lord's testimony of David.

¹⁴ But now your kingdom (Saul's) will not
endure; the LORD has sought out a man after his own heart and appointed him leader
of his people, because you have not kept the
LORD's command."   - 1 Samuel 13:14

²² After removing Saul, he made David their
king. He testified concerning him: 'I have
found David son of Jesse a man after my
own heart; he will do everything I want him
to do.'   - Acts 13:22

How did Samuel recognize this boy who would be King? Look at Samuel's own life:

> 18 But Samuel was ministering before the LORD -a boy wearing a linen ephod.
> - 1 Samuel 2:18

So here was Samuel, one who ministered unto the Lord and worshipped him as a young boy, wearing the priestly garments. Who else wore the linen ephod, the priestly garments?

> 13 When those who were carrying the ark of the LORD had taken six steps, he sacrificed a bull and a fattened calf. 14 David, wearing a linen ephod, danced before the LORD with all his might, 15 while he and the entire house of Israel brought up the ark of the LORD with shouts and the sound of trumpets.
> - 2 Samuel 6:13-15

> 26 Because God had helped the Levites who were carrying the ark of the covenant of the LORD, seven bulls and seven rams were sacrificed. 27 Now David was clothed in a robe of fine linen, as were all the Levites who were carrying the ark, and as were the singers, and Kenaniah, who was in charge of the singing of the choirs. David also wore a linen ephod.

²⁸ So all Israel brought up the ark of the covenant of the LORD with shouts, with the sounding of rams' horns and trumpets, and of cymbals, and the playing of lyres and harps. - 1 Chronicles 15:26-28

David was allowed to wear the linen ephod without penalty, because he was deemed worthy by God to wear it, it was a part of his function. Also, notice in verse 26, it says that the Lord helped the Levites carry the Ark. I believe the Lord still to this day helps his priests to carry his presence in the form of the anointing. At times it would be too heavy if the Lord did not add his strength to us to carry his Glory.

The Significance of the Priestly Garment

Let us examine the significance of the priestly garments by examining the first ones given to Aaron and his sons.

² Make sacred garments for your brother Aaron, to give him dignity and honor. ³ Tell all the skilled men to whom I have given wisdom in such matters that they are to make garments for Aaron, for his consecra-tion, so he may serve me as priest. - Exodus 28:2-3

41 **After you put these clothes on your brother Aaron and his sons, anoint and ordain them. Consecrate them so they may serve me as priests.**

42 "Make linen undergarments as a covering for the body, reaching from the waist to the thigh. **43** Aaron and his sons must wear them whenever they enter the Tent of Meeting or approach the altar to minister in the Holy Place, so that they will not incur guilt and die. "**This is to be a lasting ordinance for Aaron and his descendants.**

- Exodus 28:41-43

So what does this all mean? David was not only a worshipper, but he was a prophet, priest and King. He was not in the order of the Levitical priesthood, who received their job description from their bloodline, their family tree, and by natural inheritance. David was of a different order, a different priesthood. He was a prophetic picture of another type of priest. He was of the spiritual order of Melchizedek. Let's explore this order of Melchizedek and how it relates to both David and Jesus.

18 **Then Melchizedek king of Salem brought out bread and wine. He was priest of God Most High,** **19** **and he blessed Abram, saying,**

"Blessed be Abram by God Most High, Creator of heaven and earth.

- Genesis 14:18-19

[1] The LORD says to my Lord:
"Sit at my right hand
until I make your enemies
a footstool for your feet."

[2] The LORD will extend your mighty scepter from Zion; you will rule in the midst of your enemies.

[3] Your troops will be willing
on your day of battle.
Arrayed in holy majesty,
from the womb of the dawn
you will receive the dew of your youth.

[4] The LORD has sworn
 and will not change his mind:
 "You are a priest forever,
 in the order of Melchizedek."

- Psalm 110:1-4

[1]Every high priest is selected from among men and is appointed to represent them in matters related to God, to offer gifts and sacrifices for sins. [2] He is able to deal gently with those who are ignorant and are going astray, since he himself is subject to weakness. [3] This is why he has to offer sacrifices for his own sins, as well as for the sins of the people.

⁴ No one takes this honor upon himself; he must be called by God, just as Aaron was. ⁵ So Christ also did not take upon himself the glory of becoming a high priest. But God said to him,

"You are my Son;
today I have become your Father."

⁶ And he says in another place,

"You are a priest forever,
in the order of Melchizedek."

⁷During the days of Jesus' life on earth, he offered up prayers and petitions with loud cries and tears to the one who could save him from death, and he was heard because of his reverent submission. ⁸Although he was a son, he learned obedience from what he suffered ⁹and, once made perfect, he became the source of eternal salvation for all who obey him ¹⁰ and was designated by God to be high priest in the order of Melchizedek.   - Hebrews 5:1-10

¹⁹ We have this hope as an anchor for the soul, firm and secure. It enters the inner sanctuary behind the curtain, ²⁰ where Jesus, who went before us, has entered on our behalf. He has become a high priest forever, in the order of Melchizedek.
                    - Hebrews 6:19-20

Melchizedek the Priest

¹ This Melchizedek was king of Salem and priest of God Most High. He met Abraham returning from the defeat of the kings and blessed him, ² and Abraham gave him a tenth of everything. <u>First, his name means "king of righteousness"; then also, "king of Salem" means "king of peace."</u> ³ <u>Without father or mother, without genealogy, without beginning of days or end of life, like the Son of God he remains a priest forever.</u>

- Hebrews 7:1-3

Jesus Like Melchizedek

¹¹ If perfection could have been attained through the Levitical priesthood (for on the basis of it the law was given to the people), <u>why was there still need for another priest to come—one in the order of Melchizedek, not in the order of Aaron?</u> ¹² For when there is a change of the priesthood, there must also be a change of the law. ¹³ <u>He of whom these things are said belonged to a different tribe, and no one from that tribe has ever served at the altar.</u> ¹⁴ <u>For it is clear that our Lord descended from Judah, and in regard to that tribe Moses said nothing about priests.</u> ¹⁵ <u>And what we have said is even more clear if another priest like Melchizedek appears,</u>

16 one who has become a priest not on the basis of a regulation as to his ancestry but on the basis of the power of an indestructible life.

17 For it is declared: "You are a priest forever, in the order of Melchizedek."

18 The former regulation is set aside because it was weak and useless **19** (for the law made nothing perfect), and a better hope is introduced, by which we draw near to God.

- Hebrews 7:11-18

Read all of Hebrews 7 to get a better grasp on this subject of the priesthood that lives on forever because of the indestructible life of Jesus Christ.

David was living in another day, and was a priest of another order. David did not die when he ministered in front of the ark. Normal priests were not even allowed to go into the Holy of Holies. Only the high priest could enter and he had better be clean or he would not survive the encounter. There was no veil that kept David or the priesthood he established out of the inner sanctum where the ark resided. Just as Abraham met in person, face to face with Melchizedek and was blessed by him, so David was unafraid to meet the Lord in his sanctuary, to behold the beauty of the Lord, without the threat of the penalty of death.

> [18] **Then Melchizedek king of Salem brought out bread and wine.** **He was priest of God Most High,** - Genesis 14:18

Notice that Melchizedek brought the bread and the wine to Abraham, again a picture of Jesus, the Bread of Life, the Manna from Heaven and the new wine of the New Covenant. The bread is his body that was broken for us and the wine is his blood that was poured out for us.

> [2] **and Abraham gave him a tenth of everything. First, his name means "king of righteousness"; then also, "king of Salem" means "king of peace."** - Hebrews 7:2

His name was righteousness and peace. I believe to be a part of this priesthood; we must live that life of righteousness and peace. I believe these emanate from that secret place and transform us into his very nature. We are to be like the high priest who called us.

David also set up a ministry before the Lord for 33 years, 24 hours a day, 7 days a week. The worshippers would come in and minister unto the Lord and then rotated with the next group. They worshipped for every year that our Lord Jesus lived on the earth. To do a more in depth study of this ministry, Ray Hughes, "The Minstrel Series" is a powerful study. The musicians and singers were all trained by their fathers who were skilled in their instruments. This was a teaching and mentoring ministry that raised up sons who followed in the ways of the fathers to continue the ministry for such a lengthy period of time. I am sure there were many aspects of ministry that were passed down from father to son in the same manner and with the same vision and purpose as established by David.

David's Worship Ministry and Legacy

1 David, together with the commanders of the army, set apart some of the sons of Asaph, Heman and Jeduthun for the ministry of prophesying, accompanied by harps, lyres and cymbals. Here is the list of the men who performed this service:

2 From the sons of Asaph: Zaccur, Joseph, Nethaniah and Asarelah. The sons of Asaph were under the supervision of Asaph, who prophesied under the king's supervision.

³ As for Jeduthun, from his sons:
Gedaliah, Zeri, Jeshaiah, Shimei, Hashabiah and Mattithiah, six in all, <u>under the supervision of their father Jeduthun, who prophesied, using the harp in thanking and praising the LORD</u>.

⁴ As for Heman, from his sons:
Bukkiah, Mattaniah, Uzziel, Shubael and Jerimoth; Hananiah, Hanani, Eliathah, Giddalti and Romamti-Ezer; Joshbekashah, Mallothi, Hothir and Mahazioth. ⁵ All these were sons of Heman the king's seer. They were given him through the promises of God to exalt him. God gave Heman fourteen sons and three daughters.

⁶ <u>All these men were under the supervision of their fathers for the music of the temple of the LORD, with cymbals, lyres and harps, for the ministry at the house of God. Asaph, Jeduthun and Heman were under the supervision of the king. ⁷ Along with their relatives — all of them trained and skilled in music for the LORD -they numbered 288. ⁸Young and old alike, teacher as well as student, cast lots for their duties</u>.

- 1 Chronicles 25:1-8

Suffice it to say, their duties were to prophesy with their instruments and voices. They were set apart for prophetic ministry unto the Lord using their instruments and musical background. Also note in verse 8, that talent was in all of them, music was in their DNA. They just appointed their brothers, "young and old alike, teacher as well as student." You could have picked from any of them, their talent didn't just land them their position. I believe it was their heart and character that distinguished them for service in the house of the Lord, as it should be today in the church.

This new order of ministry unto the Lord all came from the heart of David. Not only did the Lord promise to establish his throne forever, but also to set him over his house and his kingdom.

10 and have done ever since the time I appointed leaders over my people Israel. I will also subdue all your enemies.
"'I declare to you that the LORD will build a house for you:

11 When your days are over and you go to be with your fathers, I will raise up your offspring to succeed you, one of your own sons, and I will establish his kingdom. 12 He is the one who will build a house for me, and I will establish his throne forever. 13 I will be his father, and he will be my son. I will never take my love away from him, as I took it away from your predecessor. 14 I will set

him over my house and my kingdom forever;
his throne will be established forever.' "
                        - 1 Chronicles 17:10-14

[45] But King Solomon will be blessed, and
David's throne will remain secure before the
LORD forever."   - 1 King 2:45

[6] For to us a child is born,
to us a son is given,
and the government will be on his shoulders.
And he will be called
Wonderful Counselor, Mighty God,
Everlasting Father, Prince of Peace.
[7] Of the increase of his government and
peace
there will be no end.
He will reign on David's throne
and over his kingdom,
establishing and upholding it
with justice and righteousness
from that time on and forever.
The zeal of the LORD Almighty
will accomplish this.   - Isaiah 9:6-7

And one last thing the Lord says of David:

Israel's Restoration

[11] "In that day I will restore
David's fallen tent.
I will repair its broken places,

140

restore its ruins,
<u>and build it as it used to be,</u>

- Amos 9:11

11In that day will I raise up the tabernacle of David that is fallen, and close up the breaches thereof; and I will raise up his ruins, and <u>I will build it as in the days of old</u>:

- Amos 9:11 KJV

David's worship was of an Old Testament pattern with a New Testament order and design. We will see more of this revelation unfold later. Apparently David was not a man pleaser, for the "Aaronic" priesthood would not have necessarily agreed with this new way of doing things. Are you seeing a difference and a departure that David demonstrated from his life, which did not even fit into the current pattern of the priesthood of his day? David did please God with his worship ministry, so much that God promised to restore it "as in the days of old." What is currently going on in the church, in the worship ministries and on worship platforms does not necessarily conform to the pattern as set forth in God's Word. We need to get back to the basics.

The Mercy Seat

Let us now look at the significance of the Mercy Seat of the ark as it relates to Jesus.

[10] "Have them make a chest of acacia wood—two and a half cubits long, a cubit and a half wide, and a cubit and a half high. [11] Overlay it with pure gold, both inside and out, and make a gold molding around it. [12] Cast four gold rings for it and fasten them to its four feet, with two rings on one side and two rings on the other. [13] Then make poles of acacia wood and overlay them with gold. [14] Insert the poles into the rings on the sides of the chest to carry it. [15] The poles are to remain in the rings of this ark; they are not to be removed. [16] Then put in the ark the Testimony, which I will give you.

[17] "Make an atonement cover of pure gold—two and a half cubits long and a cubit and a half wide. [18] And make two cherubim out of hammered gold at the ends of the cover. [19] Make one cherub on one end and the second cherub on the other; make the cherubim of one piece with the cover, at the two ends. [20] The cherubim are to have their wings spread upward, overshadowing the cover with them. The cherubim are to face each other, looking toward the cover. [21] Place the cover on top of the ark and put in the ark the Tes-

timony, which I will give you. ²² There, above the cover between the two cherubim that are over the ark of the Testimony, I will meet with you and give you all my commands for the Israelites.

- Exodus 25:10-22

When we think of the ark of the covenant, we assume that it is only referred to in the Old Testament. However, to get a better idea of Jesus' ministry and function as high priest, let's look at the appearance of the mercy seat in the New Testament. Notice that on the cover of the ark there are two cherubim with wings spread upward overshadowing the cover, and their faces are turned towards the cover. It is between the shadow of these wings, **(He who dwells in the shelter of the Most High will rest in the shadow of the Almighty. Psalm 91:1)** that the glory of the Lord resided as referenced in Moses' tabernacle and in Solomon's temple. Also, in verse 22, it shows the mercy seat "over the ark of the testimony" which demonstrated that mercy triumphs over judgment and the new covenant shall be seated above or covers the old covenant of the law. Let's look at the first appearance of the ark in the New Testament.

⁸ **And there were shepherds living out in the fields nearby, keeping watch over their**

flocks at night. ⁹ An angel of the Lord appeared to them, and the glory of the Lord shone around them, and they were terrified. ¹⁰ But the angel said to them, "Do not be afraid. I bring you good news of great joy that will be for all the people. ¹¹ Today in the town of David a Savior has been born to you; he is Christ the Lord. ¹² This will be a sign to you: You will find a baby wrapped in cloths and lying in a manger."

¹³ Suddenly a great company of the heavenly host appeared with the angel, praising God and saying,
¹⁴ "Glory to God in the highest,
     and on earth peace to men on whom his favor rests."

¹⁵ When the angels had left them and gone into heaven, the shepherds said to one another, "Let's go to Bethlehem and see this thing that has happened, which the Lord has told us about."

¹⁶ So they hurried off and found Mary and Joseph, and the baby, who was lying in the manger. ¹⁷ When they had seen him, they spread the word concerning what had been told them about this child, ¹⁸ and all who heard it were amazed at what the shepherds said to them. ¹⁹ But Mary treasured up all these things and pondered them in her heart. ²⁰ The shepherds returned, glorifying and praising God for all the things they had

heard and seen, which were just as they had been told.   - Luke 2:8-20

The angels were surrounding Jesus, and I believe they were covering the Lord as he lay in the manger. Consider that the shepherds were invited to this glorious display of angels with wings spread rejoicing at the birth of the Lord Jesus. Let's look at this in the context of the following verse:

> [16] Let us then approach the throne of grace with confidence, so that we may receive mercy and find grace to help us in our time of need.   - Hebrews 4:16

As you can see, the shepherds represented the common people who were allowed to come before the mercy seat, and the One who sat upon it. Let's see the second fulfillment of the ark of the covenant.

> [11] but Mary stood outside the tomb crying. As she wept, she bent over to look into the tomb [12] and saw two angels in white, seated where Jesus' body had been, one at the head and the other at the foot. - John 20:11-12

In these verses we actually see the two angels. One sat at the head of where Jesus had laid, and the other at where his feet would have been. I believe the angels spread their wings and covered the body of Jesus, and looked to the resurrection of the Lord Jesus as he perfectly fulfilled the ark of the covenant which was to meet, to dwell, to tabernacle, and to reside with his people.

> [20] which he exerted in Christ when he raised him from the dead and seated him at his right hand in the heavenly realms,
> - Ephesians 1:20

> [69] But from now on, the Son of Man will be seated at the right hand of the mighty God."
> - Luke 22:69

> [1] Since, then, you have been raised with Christ, set your hearts on things above, where Christ is seated at the right hand of God. - Colossians 3:1

This is the eternal mercy seat where Jesus is seated forever at the right hand of God. Let's now look at his function and the function of his eternal priesthood.

> [9] After this I looked and there before me was a great multitude that no one could count, from every nation, tribe, people and language, standing before the throne and in

front of the Lamb. <u>They were wearing white robes and were holding palm branches in their hands.</u> [10] And they cried out in a loud voice:

"Salvation belongs to our God,
who sits on the throne,
and to the Lamb."

[15] <u>Therefore, "they are before the throne of God and serve him day and night in his temple;</u>
<u>and he who sits on the throne will spread his tent over them.</u>
[16] Never again will they hunger;
never again will they thirst.
The sun will not beat upon them,
or any scorching heat
[17] For the Lamb at the center of the throne will be their shepherd; he will lead them to springs of living water.
And God will wipe away every tear from their eyes."
                    - Revelation 7:9-10, 15-17

[16] They called to the mountains and the rocks, "Fall on us and hide us from the face of him who sits on the throne and from the wrath of the Lamb! [17] For the great day of their wrath has come, and who can stand?"
                    - Revelation 6:16-17

For those who trust in Jesus for their salvation, mercy is extended from where Christ is seated.

He is their tender shepherd, their covering, their refuge, and the joy of their salvation. But for those who have rejected his gift of salvation is a seat of terrible judgment and the wrath of the Lamb. What an awesome picture! Jesus' ministry was to reestablish the royal priesthood, as seen in verses 10 and 15, **"Therefore, "they are before the throne of God and serve him day and night in his temple;"**

> **⁹ But you are a chosen people, a royal priesthood, a holy nation, a people belonging to God, that you may declare the praises of him who called you out of darkness into his wonderful light.**   **- 1 Peter 2:9**

> **⁶ and (Jesus) has made us to be a kingdom and priests to serve his God and Father—to him be glory and power for ever and ever!**
> **- Revelation 1:6**

Now that we have thoroughly explored the priestly role of Jesus and his seat of mercy, let us revisit David in his role.

The Key of David

What is this key of David? I believe it is the key that David birthed which is the new function and ministry of the priesthood of prophetic worship that was the predecessor of New Testament grace. David was a prototype of the prophet, priest, and king that Jesus came to establish in his church, the royal priesthood, in the order of Melchizedek.

> ⁹ But you are a chosen people, a royal priesthood, a holy nation, a people belonging to God, that you may declare the praises of him who called you out of darkness into his wonderful light.   - 1 Peter 2:9

> ⁶ and *(He, Jesus)* has made us to be a kingdom and priests to serve his God and Father—to him be glory and power for ever and ever! Amen. *emphasis mine*
> - Revelation 1:6

I also believe it is the establishing of the priesthood and the kingdom together to serve him who sits on the throne forever. And this key is in the hands of our King and High Priest Jesus Christ who is establishing a royal priesthood and kingdom forever. "The door that he opens shall be opened and the door he shuts no one can open." Isn't it a sweet release and freedom to know that the key is in the hands of our Lord Jesus, and that it is not up to us to try and pry open this door? He will open it in his time. However, there is a changing of the guard. The gate keepers of times past will make way for the new gate keepers, who will guard over this emerging way into the most Holy place where he resides, the Holy of Holies.

Chapter 7
Entering the Holy of Holies

There is a proper approach to entering the Holy of Holies, and a proper protocol that is lacking in the church and especially on the worship platforms in the American church. First of all we must know who we are and what our function is. The Old Testament and the New Testament agree as to who we are.

A Royal Priesthood

> 9 But you are a chosen people, a royal priest-hood, a holy nation, a people belonging to God, that you may declare the praises of him who called you out of darkness into his wonderful light.   - 1 Peter 2:9

> 6 you will be for me a kingdom of priests and a holy nation.' These are the words you are to speak to the Israelites."
>   - Exodus 19:6

²² Even the priests, who approach the LORD, must consecrate themselves, or the LORD will break out against them."

- Exodus 19:22

⁶ And you will be called priests of the LORD,
    you will be named ministers of our God.
    You will feed on the wealth of nations, and in their riches you will boast.

- Isaiah 61:6

⁶ and (He, Jesus) has made us to be a kingdom and priests to serve his God and Father—to him be glory and power for ever and ever! Amen. *emphasis mine*

- Revelation 1:6

¹⁰ You have made them to be a kingdom and priests to serve our God, and they will reign on the earth."
- Revelation 5:10

It is important to understand some basic mandates the Lord gave to the priesthood, in regards to how we carry out our duties unto the Lord. This is not an attempt to put people back under the Law, but to glean important truths from the original priestly ministry, in order to better understand our own.

A Lasting Ordinance for the Priesthood

17 Then the LORD said to Moses, 18 "Make a bronze basin, with its bronze stand, for washing. Place it between the Tent of Meeting and the altar, and put water in it. 19 Aaron and his sons are to wash their hands and feet with water from it.

20 Whenever they enter the Tent of Meeting, they shall wash with water so that they will not die. Also, when they approach the altar to minister by presenting an offering made to the LORD by fire, 21 they shall wash their hands and feet so that they will not die. This is to be a lasting ordinance for Aaron and his descendants for the generations to come." - Exodus 30:17-21

Jesus did not do away with the Old Testament, but came to perfectly fulfill it. This natural washing also illustrates a spiritual washing, sanctification and consecration of the heart. We will continue to see this mandate carried out in the priesthood.

12 The fire on the altar must be kept burning; it must not go out. Every morning the priest is to add firewood and arrange the burnt offering on the fire and burn the fat of the fellowship offerings on it. 13 The fire

153

must be kept burning on the altar continuously; it must not go out.
                              - Leviticus 6:12-13

²³ Moses and Aaron then went into the Tent
of Meeting. When they came out, they
blessed the people; and the glory of the
LORD appeared to all the people. ²⁴ Fire
came out from the presence of the LORD and
consumed the burnt offering and the fat portions on the altar. And when all the people
saw it, they shouted for joy and fell facedown.   - Leviticus 9:23-24

In these two passages it is important to see
the mandate of the fire that is to be kept burning, and never allowed to go out. In Leviticus
9:24, I believe we see why it was commanded
that the fire was to be kept burning. The source
of this fire came straight from the presence of
the Lord and its origin was Heaven.

I believe this fire from Heaven, is what
consumed the sacrifice and made it acceptable.
This fire came from the altar in Heaven as described in Isaiah 6: 6-7 when Isaiah cried out in
the presence of the Lord, "Woe to me for I am a
man of unclean lips..."

⁶ Then one of the seraphs flew to me with a
live coal in his hand, which he had taken

with tongs from the altar. ⁷ With it he touched my mouth and said, <u>"See, this has touched your lips; your guilt is taken away and your sin atoned for."</u> - Isaiah 6:6-7

This Heavenly fire is a type and shadow of the fire of the Holy Ghost burning within us. Our works should come from this source of heavenly fire that has been deposited within us, not from the soul which has a form of zeal that leads to a religious piety or from the flesh as we will see demonstrated in the following scripture.

Unauthorized Fire

¹ Aaron's sons Nadab and Abihu took their censers, put fire in them and added incense; and they offered unauthorized fire before the LORD, contrary to his command. ² So fire came out from the presence of the LORD and consumed them, and they died before the LORD. ³ Moses then said to Aaron, "This is what the LORD spoke of when he said:
" '<u>Among those who approach me</u>
<u>I will show myself holy;</u>
<u>in the sight of all the people</u>
<u>I will be honored</u>.' "
Aaron remained silent.   - Lev. 10:1-3

155

In this passage, we see that two of Aaron's own sons who were priests, offered up unauthorized fire, or as the King James Version calls it foreign fire, before the Lord. I believe this speaks of the severity of offering anything up that is not of Heavenly origin. And the substance of which it is made is tested through the fire. It is better to have the work of your hands and your ministry tested and tried through fire on this side of eternity, than to stand before the Lord Jesus and give an account of your life's work, and watch it go down in flames. At least now we have grace to begin again and build a lasting reward through a ministry that truly honors the Lord, and to hear the words, "Well done, thou good and faithful servant..."

> [11] For no one can lay any foundation other than the one already laid, which is Jesus Christ. [12] If any man builds on this foundation using gold, silver, costly stones, wood, hay or straw, [13] his work will be shown for what it is, because the Day will bring it to light. It will be revealed with fire, and the fire will test the quality of each man's work.
> ⁻ 1 Corinthians 3:11-13

Doing things God's way

In the following scriptures, we will discover the importance of working in accordance with the will of God.

³ Let us bring the ark of our God back to us, for we did not inquire of it during the reign of Saul." ⁴ The whole assembly agreed to do this, because it seemed right to all the people.

⁵ So David assembled all the Israelites, from the Shihor River in Egypt to Lebo Hamath, to bring the ark of God from Kiriath Jearim. ⁶ David and all the Israelites with him went to Baalah of Judah (Kiriath Jearim) to bring up from there the ark of God the LORD, who is enthroned between the cherubim — the ark that is called by the Name.

⁷ They moved the ark of God from Abinadab's house on a new cart, with Uzzah and Ahio guiding it.

⁸ David and all the Israelites were celebrating with all their might before God, with songs and with harps, lyres, tambourines, cymbals and trumpets.

⁹ When they came to the threshing floor of Kidon, Uzzah reached out his hand to steady the ark, because the oxen stumbled.

¹⁰ <u>**The LORD's anger burned against Uzzah,
and he struck him down because he had put
his hand on the ark.**</u> **So he died there before
God.** **- 1 Chronicles 13:3-9**

Notice in verse 6, the reverence brought to
the ark of God's presence, and that it is a representation of the One who sits upon the throne of
Heaven. This is not just another piece of furni-
ture but it has been specifically crafted for the
Lord himself, and it bears his name. This ark
would go out before the armies of the Lord and
the enemies were defeated in its presence.

Also, in verse 4 they believed it was a
good thing that they were doing. Of course not
all of man's ideas are best when dealing with
the things of God. In verse 4, the majority was
in agreement, yet the end result was that someone paid a costly price for this error and died.
So in verse 7 they moved the ark on a new cart.
Apparently it was shiny and had wheels and it
seemed like a good mode of transportation.

In verse 8 they were worshipping in cele-
bration and in one accord as they were bringing
the ark up in the same way that they had con-
ducted all their festivities. However, one critical mistake was made in a series of mistakes.
Uzzah reached out with the arm of flesh to
steady the ark of his presence. Legitimately, he

was doing a good thing, to keep the ark from crashing to the ground. But there was a lack of reverence for the holy things of God, specifically the ark that represented the One who sits upon the throne. Flesh shall not glory in the presence of the Lord; flesh dies in the presence of God. Flesh can not sustain or touch his glory, his presence, or his anointing. The fear of the Lord was necessary in carrying out such an important event, and I believe this reverence is still lacking in the church today.

The Ark Brought to Jerusalem

1 After David had constructed buildings for himself in the City of David, he prepared a place for the ark of God and pitched a tent for it.

2 **Then David said, "No one but the Levites may carry the ark of God, because the LORD chose them to carry the ark of the LORD and to minister before him forever."**

3 David assembled all Israel in Jerusalem to bring up the ark of the LORD to the place he had prepared for it. 4 He called together the descendants of Aaron and the Levites:

11 Then David summoned Zadok and Abiathar the priests, and Uriel, Asaiah, Joel, Shemaiah, Eliel and Amminadab the Levites. 12

He said to them, "You are the heads of the Levitical families; you and your fellow Levites are to consecrate yourselves and bring up the ark of the LORD, the God of Israel, to the place I have prepared for it. [13] It was because you, the Levites, did not bring it up the first time that the LORD our God broke out in anger against us. We did not inquire of him about how to do it in the prescribed way."

[14] So the priests and Levites consecrated themselves in order to bring up the ark of the LORD, the God of Israel. [15] And the Levites carried the ark of God with the poles on their shoulders, as Moses had commanded in accordance with the word of the LORD.

[16] David told the leaders of the Levites to appoint their brothers as singers to sing joyful songs, accompanied by musical instruments: lyres, harps and cymbals.

- 1 Chronicles 15:1-4, 11-16

Notice in 1 Chronicles 13:8 and also in 1 Chronicles 15:16 the musicians and singers were worshipping before the Lord. David had that part right, what he did not do was to approach the ark of his presence "in the prescribed way" in verse 13. How we approach the Lord and what we offer to him is as important today as it

160

was in the early days of the priesthood. If we can show honor and respect the protocol of how we approach an earthly king, how much more should we reverence the King of Glory, the King of Heaven?

A Man After God's Own Heart

There is something to be said of the legacy of David and the worship that he birthed into the earth. Listen to what God said.

Israel's Restoration

11 "In that day I will restore
David's fallen tent.
I will repair its broken places,
restore its ruins,
and build it as it used to be,
- Amos 9:11 (NIV)

11 In that day will I raise up the tabernacle of David that is fallen, and close up the breaches thereof; and I will raise up his ruins, and I will build it as in the days of old:
- Amos 9:11 (KJV)

In all of its glory, God did not say he would restore the temple of Solomon, he said he would restore the fallen tent of David. I believe this speaks of the worship and the prescribed method of serving the Lord that honored him so, the very heart of David, which was refined as pure gold before the Lord. This is what the Lord will restore in the latter day.

He also said that he would close up the breaches, the very place of intercession and standing in the gap that the Levitical priests performed before the Lord as they ministered unto him. Historically, the Levites left the house of the Lord for they could not sustain or provide for their families. So they took their ministry out into the world.

God will restore this ministry back into the house of the Lord to minister unto him again, but first, he must take the world back out of these musicians. They must consecrate themselves unto the service of the Lord.

The Lord also says that "...I will build it as in the days of old." So apparently this doesn't look anything like the pattern we see in the world or in the church. It will be done as in the beginning, as in the days of old; we must therefore conform back to the original pattern set forth in his Word. There are many good patterns of worship, and good ideas. But what is its source, the Word of God, Heaven, or the good ideas of man, with good intentions? So the

Lord must cleanse the church from its worldly pattern. If it looks like the world, (a light show or a flashy concert), smells like the world, sounds like the world, tastes like the world, it is the world, it's pattern is from the world, and its origin is earthly and of the flesh.

> **5 having a form of godliness but denying its power. Have nothing to do with them.**
> **- 2 Timothy 3:5**

I believe this is one reason there is so little power on most of the platforms in the American church, because there is so little holiness, and too much of the world; it is a mixture of good and common. It is the mixture of earth and Heaven that dilutes the pure simple power and demonstration of the gospel and why we see so few miracles and experience so little of the actual presence and Glory of God. But things are going to change...

Access to the Throne of Grace

> **16 Let us therefore come boldly unto the throne of grace that we may obtain mercy, and find grace to help in time of need.**
> **- Hebrews 4:16**

The veil was rent in two! We now have access to the Holy of Holies, but not all can enter. First of all, they do not approach him as priests and ministers of the Lord, and secondly they do not approach him in the prescribed way. Though the way is made unto us through the blood of the Lamb, we must press forward past performance, past our own talent, and we must come before him in a consecrated way. In Exodus 30:19-21, it says:

> "[19] Aaron and his sons are to wash their hands and feet with water from it. [20] Whenever they enter the Tent of Meeting, they shall wash with water so that they will not die. Also, when they approach the altar to minister by presenting an offering made to the LORD by fire, [21] they shall wash their hands and feet so that they will not die. This is to be a lasting ordinance for Aaron and his descendants for the generations to come." — Exodus 30:19-21

We must clean our hands of the ways of the world, and our feet of the paths of the world, and ascend unto the hill of the Lord with clean hands and a pure heart.

[3] Who may ascend the hill of the LORD?
Who may stand in his holy place?

⁴ He who has clean hands and a pure heart, who does not lift up his soul to an idol or swear by what is false.

- Psalm 24:3-4

Ezekiel's Standard for the Priesthood

As we explore the mandates of the priesthood, we must revisit a passage that we have already discussed, as it is most applicable here. There was a separation even amongst the priesthood as to those who ministered to the people and those who were allowed to come near unto the Lord.

¹⁰ " 'The Levites who went far from me when Israel went astray and who wandered from me after their idols must bear the consequences of their sin. ¹¹ They may serve in my sanctuary, having charge of the gates of the temple and serving in it; they may slaughter the burnt offerings and sacrifices for the people and stand before the people and serve them. ¹² But because they served them in the presence of their idols and made the house of Israel fall into sin, therefore I have sworn with uplifted hand that they must bear the consequences of their sin, declares the Sovereign LORD.

165

¹³ They are not to come near to serve me as priests or come near any of my holy things or my most holy offerings; they must bear the shame of their detestable practices. ¹⁴ Yet I will put them in charge of the duties of the temple and all the work that is to be done in it.

¹⁵ " 'But the priests, who are Levites and descendants of Zadok and who faithfully carried out the duties of my sanctuary when the Israelites went astray from me, are to come near to minister before me; they are to stand before me to offer sacrifices of fat and blood, declares the Sovereign LORD. ¹⁶ They alone are to enter my sanctuary; they alone are to come near my table to minister before me and perform my service. ²³ They are to teach my people the difference between the holy and the common and show them how to distinguish between the unclean and the clean.

²⁴ " 'In any dispute, the priests are to serve as judges and decide it according to my ordinances. They are to keep my laws and my decrees for all my appointed feasts, and they are to keep my Sabbaths holy.
                    - Ezekiel 44:10-16, 23-24

The Levites performed their priestly duties in the presence of their idols. Have you ever wondered why the glory may come through one and not another? Just like the priests performing their duties in the presence of idols, I believe performance on the platform to be idolatry before the Lord. Performance is rooted in pride, in getting the glory, the limelight, the applause, and the adoration of the people.

> 8 "I am the LORD; that is my name!
> I will not give my glory to another
> or my praise to idols.   - Isaiah 42:8

In Exodus 32:1-8, the people fashioned a golden calf which they thought to be a representation of their god, and they began to celebrate by worshipping, dancing, and singing before their god, but it was merely an idol.

Lesson: Be careful that what your hands have fashioned, your ministry, your talent, etc. has not become a golden calf to you. You think you are worshipping the Lord yet it turns out to be a golden calf.

The Glory of the Former House

> 13 The trumpeters and singers joined in unison, as with one voice, to give praise and thanks to the LORD. Accompanied by trumpets, cymbals and other instruments, they

raised their voices in praise to the LORD
and sang:
     "He is good;
     his love endures forever."
Then the temple of the LORD was filled
with a cloud, [14] and the priests could not
perform their service because of the cloud,
for the glory of the LORD filled the temple
of God.   - 2 Chronicles 5:13-14

The Dedication of the Temple

[1] When Solomon finished praying, fire came
down from heaven and consumed the burnt
offering and the sacrifices, and the glory of
the LORD filled the temple. [2] The priests
could not enter the temple of the LORD because the glory of the LORD filled it. [3] When
all the Israelites saw the fire coming down
and the glory of the LORD above the temple,
they knelt on the pavement with their faces
to the ground, and they worshiped and gave
thanks to the LORD, saying,
     "He is good; his love endures forever."
                    - 2 Chronicles 7:1-3

Are we seeing this kind of glory in the
church today? The glory of the modern church
does not even come close to rivaling that of the
former house, yet the Word of God says it will
surpass it.

168

⁹ The glory of this latter house shall be greater than of the former, saith the LORD of hosts: and in this place will I give peace, saith the LORD of hosts.

- Haggai 2:9 KJV

Seek His Face:

Our next function of worship in the Holy of Holies is to seek his face. We see this in the heart of David as well as Moses.

⁸ My heart says of you, "Seek his face!"
Your face, LORD, I will seek.

- Psalms 27:8

² I have seen you in the sanctuary
and beheld your power and your glory.

- Psalm 63:2

¹⁸But we all, with open face beholding as in a glass the glory of the Lord, are changed into the same image from glory to glory, even as by the Spirit of the Lord.

- 2 Corinthians 3:18 KJV

¹⁸And we, who with unveiled faces all reflect the Lord's glory, are being transformed into his likeness with ever-increasing glory, which comes from the Lord, who is the Spirit.

- 2 Corinthians 3:18

The Glory of the New Covenant

⁷ Now if the ministry that brought death, which was engraved in letters on stone, came with glory, so that the Israelites could not look steadily at the face of Moses because of its glory, fading though it was, ⁸ will not the ministry of the Spirit be even more glorious? ⁹ If the ministry that condemns men is glorious, how much more glorious is the ministry that brings righteousness! ¹⁰ For what was glorious has no glory now in comparison with the surpassing glory.

¹¹ And if what was fading away came with glory, how much greater is the glory of that which lasts!

¹² Therefore, since we have such a hope, we are very bold. ¹³ We are not like Moses, who would put a veil over his face to keep the Israelites from gazing at it while the radiance was fading away. ¹⁴ But their minds were made dull, for to this day the same veil remains when the old covenant is read. It has not been removed, because only in Christ is it taken away. ¹⁵ Even to this day when Moses is read, a veil covers their hearts.

¹⁶ But whenever anyone turns to the Lord, the veil is taken away. ¹⁷ Now the Lord is the Spirit, and where the Spirit of the Lord is, there is freedom. ¹⁸ And we, who with

unveiled faces all reflect the Lord's glory, are being transformed into his likeness with ever-increasing glory, which comes from the Lord, who is the Spirit.
- 2 Corinthians 3:7-18

[12] Now we see but a poor reflection as in a mirror; then we shall see face to face. Now I know in part; then I shall know fully, even as I am fully known.
- 1 Corinthians 13:12

[22] Do not merely listen to the word, and so deceive yourselves. Do what it says. [23] Anyone who listens to the word but does not do what it says is like a man who looks at his face in a mirror [24] and, after looking at himself, goes away and immediately forgets what he looks like.   - James 1:22-24

What is the purpose of the mirror? We must look into the mirror of his Word, into the face of who he is, and when we behold who he is, then we are changed into the very likeness of that which we behold, the image of the Son. We must see ourselves as the bride of Christ, we must behold him and his likeness so that he is reflected in our countenance, for the veil has been removed from us that we may see him face to face.

Both Moses and David sought the face of the Lord. It says that God spoke with Moses face to face. David was a man after God's own heart. So many times in the Psalms he says to seek the face of the Lord.

A Revelation of the Face of the Lord

[12] I turned around to see the voice that was speaking to me. And when I turned I saw seven golden lampstands, [13] and among the lampstands was someone "like a son of man," dressed in a robe reaching down to his feet and with a golden sash around his chest.

[14] His head and hair were white like wool, as white as snow, and his eyes were like blazing fire. [15] His feet were like bronze glowing in a furnace, and his voice was like the sound of rushing waters. [16] In his right hand he held seven stars, and out of his mouth came a sharp double-edged sword. His face was like the sun shining in all its brilliance.

[17] When I saw him, I fell at his feet as though dead. Then he placed his right hand on me and said: "Do not be afraid. I am the First and the Last. [18] I am the Living One; I was dead, and behold I am alive for ever and

ever! And I hold the keys of death and Hades. - Revelation 1:12-18

As I meditate upon these scriptures, I have imagined his face and pressed through in worship. The Lord gave us a visible representation of the face of the Lord, and as I gaze upon him, he is altogether lovely. This is a very beautiful picture. I believe the imagination is the natural of what the prophetic senses are in the spiritual. And, I believe it to be a key in unlocking the spiritual sight through faith. If seeing is believing, then believing is seeing. Also as we peer into who the Lord Jesus is, we look into the mirror of his Word which reveals the imprint of who he was when he dwelt among us. There is glory in the pages of what he said and what he did. Sometimes you can just feel the Glory come right off the pages, no other commentary necessary, just him and the revelation of who he is, the great I AM.

If I am to look as he looked, I am also to do the very same works and greater than he did while he occupied the earth. I believe the greater works really means that there is a multiplication of the people operating in the Glory he left for us, not just one man, but many sons and daughters showing forth his Glory. He left his pattern that we may follow in his footsteps.

173

[19] Jesus gave them this answer: "I tell you the truth, the Son can do nothing by himself; he can do only what he sees his Father doing, because whatever the Father does the Son also does.   - John 5:19

[24] "Father, I want those you have given me to be with me where I am, and to see my glory, the glory you have given me because you loved me before the creation of the world.
- John 17:24

It was Jesus prayer to the Father that we see him and that his Glory would be revealed to us and through us.

The Vine and the Branches

[1] "I am the true vine, and my Father is the gardener. [2] He cuts off every branch in me that bears no fruit, while every branch that does bear fruit he prunes so that it will be even more fruitful. [3] You are already clean because of the word I have spoken to you. [4] Remain in me, and I will remain in you. No branch can bear fruit by itself; it must remain in the vine. Neither can you bear fruit unless you remain in me.

[5] "I am the vine; you are the branches. If a man remains in me and I in him, he will

174

bear much fruit; apart from me you can do nothing.

6 If anyone does not remain in me, he is like a branch that is thrown away and withers; such branches are picked up, thrown into the fire and burned. 7 If you remain in me and my words remain in you, ask whatever you wish, and it will be given you. 8 This is to my Father's glory, that you bear much fruit, showing yourselves to be my disciples.
- John 15:1-7

It brings the Father Glory when the sons and daughters look just like the Son, and bear his fruit. His fruit attests to who he is and who sent him, the Father. When we bear much fruit for him, we show ourselves to be his true disciples.

Crossing the Final Threshold of the Holy of Holies

As a final protocol, we come only to the Father through the blood of Jesus.

6 Jesus answered, "I am the way and the truth and the life. No one comes to the Father except through me.   - John 14:6

So who did he say he was, and if he is actually the way to the Father, how do we approach the Father through him? Jesus answered this with the truth, though many could not accept this truth and fell away from him.

⁴⁸ I am the bread of life. ⁴⁹ Your forefathers ate the manna in the desert, yet they died. ⁵⁰ But here is the bread that comes down from heaven, which a man may eat and not die. ⁵¹ I am the living bread that came down from heaven. If anyone eats of this bread, he will live forever. This bread is my flesh, which I will give for the life of the world."

⁵² Then the Jews began to argue sharply among themselves, "How can this man give us his flesh to eat?"

⁵³ Jesus said to them, "I tell you the truth, unless you eat the flesh of the Son of Man and drink his blood, you have no life in you. ⁵⁴ Whoever eats my flesh and drinks my blood has eternal life, and I will raise him up at the last day. ⁵⁵ For my flesh is real food and my blood is real drink. ⁵⁶ Whoever eats my flesh and drinks my blood remains in me, and I in him. ⁵⁷ Just as the living Father sent me and I live because of the Father, so the one who feeds on me will live because of me. ⁵⁸ This is the bread that came down from heaven. Your forefathers ate

manna and died, but he who feeds on this
bread will live forever."   - John 6:48-58

[19] And he took bread, gave thanks and broke
it, and gave it to them, saying, "This is my
body given for you; do this in remembrance
of me." [20] In the same way, after the supper
he took the cup, saying, "This cup is the new
covenant in my blood, which is poured out
for you.   - Luke 22:19 -20

Jesus was the veil that was rent in two; he
is our passage into the very place that was
forbidden from all to come into, except the high
priest, once a year. Though this place was
beautifully appointed and full of glory, no one
was able to even see its beauty, until the way
was made, through the broken body of Jesus.
When we tear the bread in two, it is the actual
representation of the body that was broken for
us that we may have access into the most holy
place of all, the Holy of Holies.

[19] Therefore, brothers, since we have confi-
dence to enter the Most Holy Place by the
blood of Jesus, [20] by a new and living way
opened for us through the curtain, that is,
his body,   - Hebrews 10:19-20

The Holy of Holies is also a representation of the Throne Room of God, the Temple of God in Isaiah 6.

¹ In the year that King Uzziah died, <u>I saw the Lord seated on a throne, high and exalted, and the train of his robe filled the temple.</u> - Isaiah 6:1

¹¹ <u>Then David gave his son Solomon the plans</u> for the portico of the temple, its buildings, its storerooms, its upper parts, its inner rooms and the place of atonement. ¹² <u>He gave him the plans of all that the Spirit had put in his mind for the courts of the temple of the LORD and all the surrounding rooms,</u> for the treasuries of the temple of God and for the treasuries for the dedicated things. - 1 Chronicles 28:11-12

⁵<u>They serve at a sanctuary that is a copy and shadow of what is in heaven. This is why Moses was warned when he was about to build the tabernacle: "See to it that you make everything according to the pattern shown you on the mountain."</u> - Hebrews 8:5

⁴⁴ "Our forefathers had the tabernacle of the Testimony with them in the desert. <u>It had been made as God directed Moses, according to the pattern he had seen.</u> - Acts 7:44

⁹ Make this tabernacle and all its furnishings exactly like the pattern I will show you.
                                    - Exodus 25:9

³⁰ "Set up the tabernacle according to the plan shown you on the mountain.
                                   - Exodus 26:30

We have already seen that the Holy of Holies was fashioned after a heavenly example of the very Throne Room of God, the Temple of God, with an altar before the Lord, and it was fashioned by human hands in accordance to the heavenly pattern? Not only did Moses receive the heavenly blueprints for the tabernacle of Moses, but David also received the blueprints for the temple that would be built by his son Solomon. And the Father made a way into the most holy place through the very body of his own son. Does this speak of how much he wants us to go in there with him?

²³ Yet a time is coming and has now come when the true worshipers will worship the Father in spirit and truth, for they are the kind of worshipers the Father seeks.
                                      - John 4:23

² In my Father's house are many rooms; if it were not so, I would have told you. I am going there to prepare a place for you. ³ And if

179

I go and prepare a place for you, <u>I will come back and take you to be with me that you also may be where I am. 4 You know the way to the place where I am going.</u>"

- John 14:2-4

I believe one of the rooms where Jesus resides is in the Holy of Holies, the worship room of Heaven. He said that we could be where he is, and where is he? He is seated in heavenly places, seated at the right hand of the Father.

> 6 And hath raised us up together, and <u>made us sit together in heavenly places in Christ Jesus:</u>   - Ephesians 2:6

> 1 Since, then, you have been raised with Christ, <u>set your hearts on things above, where Christ is seated at the right hand of God</u>.   - Colossians 3:1

> 20 which he exerted in Christ when he raised him from the dead and <u>seated him at his right hand in the heavenly realms,</u>
> - Ephesians 1:20

> 9 Therefore <u>God exalted him to the highest place</u> and gave him the name that is above every name, 10 that at the name of Jesus every knee should bow, in heaven and on earth and under the earth, 11 and every

tongue confess that Jesus Christ is Lord, to
the glory of God the Father.
                              - Philippians 2:9-11

We are called to go there regularly
through worship and prayer, because we are
positionally seated with him even now in the
heavenly places. We have access to that place;
now let that door be opened to us. Notice who
holds the keys of David, the one who worshipped the Lord with his whole heart, and the
one whose tabernacle will be restored in Amos
9:11.

> 7 "To the angel of the church in Philadelphia
> write:
> These are the words of him who is holy and
> true, who holds the key of David. What he
> opens no one can shut, and what he shuts no
> one can open. 8 I know your deeds. <u>See, I
> have placed before you an open door that no
> one can shut.</u> I know that you have little
> strength, yet you have kept my word and
> have not denied my name.
>   - Revelation 3:7-8

Jesus holds the key of David, to the restoration of the tabernacle of David, the worship
that honored God. And He has opened the door
before us, and it remains open for us anytime

we dare to enter to worship him. He is the way and the door into the Holy of Holies, made by the sacrifice of his body and blood shed for us.

Worthy is the Lamb! Hallelujah!

Chapter 8
The Glory Returns

When the Pattern is Right

The Lord spoke something very clearly to me. I already knew this to be true, but he spoke it anyway. He said, "When the pattern is right, the glory will come!" That statement just rolls through my spirit. Part of the purpose of this book is to point out that the pattern we have so readily accepted in the church is that of the world's and the enemy's deception, and does not resemble the blueprint left in the Word of God. Of course the blueprint is not complete without its architect, Jesus Christ. He knew the pattern; he came from the pattern. Let's look at what the Lord said when he saw the religious system's departure from the pattern.

Jesus at the Temple

12 Jesus entered the temple area and drove out all who were buying and selling there. He overturned the tables of the money changers and the benches of those selling doves. 13 "It is written," he said to them, 'My

house will be called a house of prayer,' but you are making it a 'den of robbers.'

¹⁴The blind and the lame came to him at the temple, and he healed them.

- Matthew 21:12-14

Jesus is referring to this scripture found in Isaiah.

⁶ And foreigners who bind themselves to the LORD
   to serve him,
   to love the name of the LORD,
   and to worship him,
   all who keep the Sabbath without desecrating it
   and who hold fast to my covenant-

⁷ these I will bring to my holy mountain
   and give them joy in my house of prayer.
   Their burnt offerings and sacrifices
   will be accepted on my altar;
   for my house will be called
   a house of prayer for all nations."

- Isaiah 56:6-7

If Jesus were to visit his church today, would he say the same thing? What would he say to those who merchandize the anointing to further their own ministries and stature? What would he think of the lack of prayer, the kind where the blind and lame are truly healed? Was he, through us, able to reach out his hands to restore them? Or what would he say of the form of godliness and religiosity, like what he saw when he first came into the earth that denies the power of God? Jesus' prayer was that when he returned he would still find "Faith" in the earth.

> 7 And will not God bring about justice for his chosen ones, who cry out to him day and night? Will he keep putting them off? 8 I tell you, he will see that they get justice, and quickly. <u>However, when the Son of Man comes, will he find faith on the earth?</u>"
>
> 9 To some who were confident of their own righteousness and looked down on everybody else, Jesus told this parable:
> - Luke 18:7-9

Which pattern is right?

God left the blueprints of Heaven in the hands of several trustworthy men. Understand that the earthly pattern was a mere representation of the heavenly pattern which reveals Jesus "the tabernacle that dwelled among us" in every facet. Let's look at the first pattern. This pattern was given directly to Moses when he ascended the mountain to receive the 10 commandments.

> [8] "Then have them make a sanctuary for me, and I will dwell among them. [9] Make this tabernacle and all its furnishings exactly like the pattern I will show you.
>
> - Exodus 25:8

> [40] See that you make them according to the pattern shown you on the mountain.
>
> - Exodus 25:40

> [4] This is how the lamp stand was made: It was made of hammered gold—from its base to its blossoms. The lamp stand was made exactly like the pattern the LORD had shown Moses.
>
> - Numbers 8:4

> [44] "Our forefathers had the tabernacle of the Testimony with them in the desert. <u>It had been made as God directed Moses, according to the pattern he had seen.</u> [45] Having received the tabernacle, our fathers under Joshua brought it with them when they took the land from the nations God drove out before them. It remained in the land until the time of David,
>
> - Acts 7:44-45

> [5] <u>They serve at a sanctuary that is a copy and shadow of what is in heaven.</u> This is why

Moses was warned when he was about to build the tabernacle: "<u>See to it that you make everything according to the pattern shown you on the mountain.</u>" 6 But the ministry Jesus has received is as superior to theirs as the covenant of which he is mediator is superior to the old one, and it is founded on better promises.

- Hebrews 8:5-6

The Lord is very specific about Moses following the pattern because it is an exact replica of the temple in Heaven. Let's look at Isaiah's encounter with the Lord in the temple of Heaven.

1 In the year that King Uzziah died, <u>I saw the Lord seated on a throne, high and exalted, and the train of his robe filled the temple.</u> 2 Above him were seraphs, each with six wings: With two wings they covered their faces, with two they covered their feet, and with two they were flying. 3 And they were calling to one another:

"Holy, holy, holy is the LORD Almighty;

the whole earth is full of his glory."

4 At the sound of their voices the <u>doorposts and thresholds shook and the temple</u> was filled with smoke.

⁵ "Woe to me!" I cried. "I am ruined! For I am a man of unclean lips, and I live among a people of unclean lips, and my eyes have seen the King, the LORD Almighty."

⁶ Then one of the seraphs flew to me with a live coal in his hand, which he had taken with tongs from the altar. ⁷ With it he touched my mouth and said, "See, this has touched your lips; your guilt is taken away and your sin atoned for."

- Isaiah 6:1-6

Did you notice something interesting in verse 6? There is a fire that burns on an altar with live coals burning on it, "hot enough" for the angel to use tongs to extract them? There were also doorposts (gates) and thresholds (separations from one section to another) in the temple. Also, it says that Isaiah saw the Lord seated on a throne and his robe filled the temple. The throne room of Heaven and the temple of Heaven are one in the same.

¹² The fire on the altar must be kept burning; it must not go out. Every morning the priest is to add firewood and arrange the burnt offering on the fire and burn the fat of the fellowship offerings on it. ¹³ The fire must be kept burning on the altar continuously; it must not go out.

²³ Moses and Aaron then went into the Tent of Meeting. When they came out, they blessed the people; and the glory of the LORD appeared to all the people. ²⁴ <u>Fire came out from the presence of the LORD and consumed the burnt offering and the fat portions on the altar. And when all the people saw it, they shouted for joy and fell facedown.</u>

Leviticus 9:23-24

Didn't you think it was strange that the Lord would command them to never allow the fire to burn out? Why do you suppose, Aaron's sons Nadab and Abihu died instantly when they offered strange or foreign fire before the Lord? The key is found in verse 24 where it says that fire came from the presence of the Lord in Heaven, to consume the very first sacrifice. I believe this fire from Heaven came from the altar found in Isaiah 6 where the angel placed the live coal to Isaiah's lips, and declared to Isaiah, **"With it he touched my mouth and said, "See, this has touched your lips; your guilt is taken away and your sin atoned for."** It was this fire from the altar of Heaven that came out of the presence of the Lord and consumed the first sacrifice that was never to be allowed to die out. He is saying the same thing to us today. John the Baptist spoke about this fire, into which we were baptized, in the following verse:

> [11] I baptize you with water for repentance. But after me will come one who is more powerful than I, whose sandals I am not fit to carry. He will baptize you with the Holy Spirit and with fire.   - Matthew 3:11

This is the same fire by which we obtain the promises of God to do greater works than even Jesus while He was on the earth.

> [12] I tell you the truth, anyone who has faith in me will do what I have been doing. He will do even greater things than these, because I am going to the Father.
> - John 14:12

Jesus even speaks of the temple, first the earthly temple and then the temple in Heaven.

> [16] "Woe to you, blind guides! You say, 'If anyone swears by the temple, it means nothing; but if anyone swears by the gold of the temple, he is bound by his oath.' [17] You blind fools! Which is greater: the gold, or the <u>temple that makes the gold sacred</u>? [18] You also say, 'If anyone swears by the altar,

it means nothing; but if anyone swears by the gift on it, he is bound by his oath.'

[19] You blind men! Which is greater: the gift, or <u>the altar that makes the gift sacred</u>? [20] Therefore, he who <u>swears by the altar swears by it and by everything on it.</u> [21] And he who <u>swears by the temple swears by it and by the one who dwells in it</u>. [22] And he who <u>swears by heaven swears by God's throne and by the one who sits on it</u>.

- Matthew 23:16-22

Jesus testifies of Himself

"[6] <u>I tell you that one greater than the temple is here</u>." - Matthew 12:6

Jesus confronted the religious system of his day because it did not resemble the pattern originally handed down to man. Paul gives us clear instruction concerning this.

[2] <u>Do not conform any longer to the pattern of this world,</u> but be transformed by the renewing of your mind. Then you will be able to test and approve what God's will is—his good, pleasing and perfect will.

- Romans 12:2

Another Blueprint

David, whose heart's desire was to build a house for his Father's name, delivered the blueprints from Heaven to his son Solomon whom God had chosen for the task of building his temple.

> [10] Consider now, for the LORD has chosen you to build a temple as a sanctuary. Be strong and do the work." [11] <u>Then David gave his son Solomon the plans for the portico of the temple, its buildings, its storerooms, its upper parts, its inner rooms and the place of atonement</u>.

> [12] <u>He gave him the plans of all that the Spirit had put in his mind for the courts of the temple of the LORD and all the surrounding rooms, for the treasuries of the temple of God and for the treasuries for the dedicated things.</u> [13] He gave him instructions for the divisions of the priests and Levites, and for all the work of serving in the temple of the LORD, as well as for all the articles to be used in its service.

> [14] He designated the weight of gold for all the gold articles to be used in various kinds of service, and the weight of silver for all the silver articles to be used in various kinds of service: [15] the weight of gold for the gold lampstands and their lamps, with the

weight for each lampstand and its lamps; and the weight of silver for each silver lampstand and its lamps, according to the use of each lampstand; 16 the weight of gold for each table for consecrated bread; the weight of silver for the silver tables;

17 the weight of pure gold for the forks, sprinkling bowls and pitchers; the weight of gold for each gold dish; the weight of silver for each silver dish; 18 and the weight of the refined gold for the altar of incense. He also gave him the plan for the chariot, that is, the cherubim of gold that spread their wings and shelter the ark of the covenant of the LORD.

19 "All this," David said, "I have in writing from the hand of the LORD upon me, and he gave me understanding in all the details of the plan."   - 1 Chronicles 28: 10-19

Even though David was not allowed to build the temple which was in his heart to do so, he amassed the most extravagant materials from which his son Solomon would build the Temple. I believe that the gold, lining the inner sanctuary of the temple, represented the purity of David's heart for the Lord, a heart of gold that had been refined in the fire.

Gifts for Building the Temple

¹ Then King David said to the whole assembly: "My son Solomon, the one whom God has chosen, is young and inexperienced. <u>The task is great, because this palatial structure is not for man but for the LORD God.</u> ² <u>With all my resources I have provided for the temple of my God—gold for the gold work, silver for the silver, bronze for the bronze, iron for the iron and wood for the wood, as well as onyx for the settings, turquoise, stones of various colors, and all kinds of fine stone and marble—all of these in large quantities.</u>

³ <u>Besides, in my devotion to the temple of my God I now give my personal treasures of gold and silver for the temple of my God, over and above everything I have provided for this holy temple:</u> ⁴ three thousand talents of gold (gold of Ophir) and seven thousand talents of refined silver, for the overlaying of the walls of the buildings, ⁵ for the gold work and the silver work, and for all the work to be done by the craftsmen. Now, who is willing to consecrate himself today to the LORD?"   - 1 Chronicles 29:1-5

Incidentally, if David can ask for an offering unto the Lord, why can't we?

One Last Pattern of the Temple

10 "Son of man, <u>describe the temple to the people of Israel, that they may be ashamed of their sins. Let them consider the plan,</u> 11 <u>and if they are ashamed of all they have done, make known to them the design of the temple—its arrangement, its exits and entrances—its whole design and all its regulations and laws. Write these down before them so that they may be faithful to its design and follow all its regulations.</u>

12 "This is the law of the temple: All the surrounding area on top of the mountain will be most holy. <u>Such is the law of the temple.</u>
- Ezekiel 43:10-12

This pattern as described in Ezekiel 40-47 is a pattern of the temple that has yet to be constructed. However, the Lord still gave this vision to Ezekiel that he would impart it to the people. Isn't it interesting that in the latter part of verse 11, he says, **"Write these down before them so that they may be faithful to its design and follow all its regulations."** This blueprint, of the yet to be constructed temple, has been given to us that we might be faithful to its design despite the fact that we have no physical place in which to apply it. I believe this blueprint also provides the spiritual order for worship by which we are to minister unto the Lord.

Is the Lord not still giving revelation of the Heavenly temple to his people?

Come up into the Glory of the Lord

Let us also examine Moses' testimony of the Glory of the Lord. Though he was not a born again man, he predated the coming of our Savior and Redeemer; he was allowed to come up close and personal to meet with God face to face (Ex 33:11) in all of his Glory.

> [9] Moses and Aaron, Nadab and Abihu, and the seventy elders of Israel went up [10] and saw the God of Israel. Under his feet was something like a pavement made of sapphire, clear as the sky itself. [11] <u>But God did not raise his hand against these leaders of the Israelites; they saw God, and they ate and drank</u>. [12] The LORD said to Moses, "Come up to me on the mountain and stay here, and I will give you the tablets of stone, with the law and commands I have written for their instruction."
>
> [13] Then Moses set out with Joshua his aide, and Moses went up on the mountain of God. [14] He said to the elders, "Wait here for us until we come back to you. Aaron and Hur are with you, and anyone involved in a dispute can go to them."

[15] When Moses went up on the mountain, the cloud covered it, [16] and the glory of the LORD settled on Mount Sinai. For six days the cloud covered the mountain, and on the seventh day the LORD called to Moses from within the cloud. [17] To the Israelites the glory of the LORD looked like a consuming fire on top of the mountain. [18] Then Moses entered the cloud as he went on up the mountain. And he stayed on the mountain forty days and forty nights.

- Exodus 24:9-18

The Tent of Meeting

[7] Now Moses used to take a tent and pitch it outside the camp some distance away, calling it the "tent of meeting." Anyone inquiring of the LORD would go to the tent of meeting outside the camp. [8] And whenever Moses went out to the tent, all the people rose and stood at the entrances to their tents, watching Moses until he entered the tent.

[9] As Moses went into the tent, the pillar of cloud would come down and stay at the entrance, while the LORD spoke with Moses. [10] Whenever the people saw the pillar of cloud standing at the entrance to the tent, they all stood and worshipped, each at the entrance to his tent. [11] The LORD would

speak to Moses face to face, as a man speaks with his friend. Then Moses would return to the camp, but his young aide Joshua son of Nun did not leave the tent.

- Exodus 33:7-11

The high calling of the worship leader is spelled out in Moses' life. Moses went up into the Glory of the Lord, met with him face to face, and when he descended to where the people were, the remnants of that Glory remained on his face.

The difference between the 2nd and the 3rd day ministry is this: 2nd day leaders are ministering out of their anointings, talents, charisma, personalities, and abilities. It seems that God anoints them even though when they step out of any given service or times of ministry, some still have the capacity to fall back into willful or hidden sin. How can God anoint one of these so called "leaders" or seemingly approve of their sinful lifestyles? (Now please don't misunderstand me; there are many holy men and women in ministry today.) It's because God anoints them for the purpose of reaching the lost sheep on the back row, which will die if they don't receive a touch from God. It is for the people's sake that he anoints the ministers even when their lives do not measure up to his standards in private.

3rd day leaders go up into the Glory of God, are transformed in the Glory, and when they minister to the people, they have remnants of the Glory all over them just like Moses. They minister out of the overflow of the Glory and the people get it. To carry the Glory, they must have a life of holiness, for as we have seen in previous chapters, all flesh will die in that Glory, in the Presence of the Lord. You can not have the Glory of God apart from the Holiness of God, they are inseparable. Let me say it again, "**You cannot have His Glory without His Holiness.**" And that is the difference between those who simply minister to the people and those who also carry the Glory, the Holiness sets them apart. You cannot go into the Glory of God and not be changed from glory to glory as in Paul's letter to the Corinthians.

18But we all, with open face beholding as in a glass the glory of the Lord, <u>are changed into the same image from glory to glory,</u> even as by the Spirit of the Lord.
- 2 Corinthians 3:18

And look at verse 10 of Exodus 33.

¹⁰ Whenever the people saw the pillar of cloud standing at the entrance to the tent, they all stood and worshipped, each at the entrance to his tent. – Exodus 33:10

The people worship when the presence of the Glory is upon the minister. When the worshipper or priest ministers unto the Lord in the Glory, the people are brought into that worship, and all experience the Glory and the presence of the Lord. Will people say of you, "He has been with Jesus!"

When the Pattern is Right, the Glory Will Come!

We already saw the reaction of the people at the first sacrifice given in the tabernacle of Moses. They had been faithful to do everything according to the pattern the Lord had given them. Here is the fruit.

The Glory of the Lord

³⁴Then the cloud covered the tent of meeting, and the glory of the LORD filled the tabernacle. ³⁵And Moses was not able to enter the tent of meeting because the cloud settled on it, and the glory of the LORD filled the tabernacle. – Exodus 40:34-35

24 Fire came out from the presence of the LORD and consumed the burnt offering and the fat portions on the altar. <u>And when all the people saw it, they shouted for joy and fell facedown.</u>   - Leviticus 9:24

Sounds like one minute they were jumping and rejoicing, and the next minute they fell prostrate before the Lord. I wonder why the different response? Consider this passage and note the similarities.

8 Each of the four living creatures had six wings and was covered with eyes all around, even under his wings. Day and night they never stop saying: "Holy, holy, holy is the Lord God Almighty, who was, and is, and is to come." **9** Whenever the living creatures give glory, honor and thanks to him who sits on the throne and who lives for ever and ever,

10 the twenty-four elders fall down before him who sits on the throne, and worship him who lives for ever and ever. They lay their crowns before the throne and say:
11 "You are worthy, our Lord and God,
to receive glory and honor and power,
for you created all things,
and by your will they were created
and have their being."
                    - Revelation 4:8-11

¹³Then I heard every creature in heaven and on earth and under the earth and on the sea, and all that is in them, singing:
"To him who sits on the throne and to the Lamb
be praise and honor and glory and power, for ever and ever!"

¹⁴The four living creatures said, "Amen," and the elders fell down and worshipped.
- Revelation 5:13-14

I believe the Glory was manifested in their presence and they went from rejoicing to awe-struck worship before the Lord in the Splendor and Majesty and Glory of the Lord. When we declare who he is, he is a demonstrator of the word spoken of him, the truth of his holiness and his Glory. Once the angels and the elders declared that "he is Holy", I believe our God in this eternal glimpse of Heaven demonstrated the power of his awesome wonder, and the elders went from rejoicing to completely undone and awestruck at such a magnificent display of his Glory. He will be revealing the magnificence of his Glory to more and more of his Glory for all eternity. Just when we think he has shown us all he is, there he goes again, blowing the lid off what we thought we knew of him. The angels never tire day and night of declaring how holy and glorious and worthy he is, and there go the elders again, prostrate before the Lord with their crowns in their hands. And so will we when we finally get to see him in all of his Majesty. That is more than I can even fathom here!

Let's look at the fulfillment of the second pattern that was given and obediently constructed according to that which was given to David.

> [1] Then Solomon said, "The LORD has said that he would dwell in a dark cloud; [2] I have built a magnificent temple for you, a place for you to dwell forever."
>
> [3] While the whole assembly of Israel was standing there, the king turned around and blessed them. [4] Then he said: "Praise be to the LORD, the God of Israel, who with his hands has fulfilled what he promised with his mouth to my father David. For he said, [5] 'Since the day I brought my people out of Egypt, I have not chosen a city in any tribe of Israel to have a temple built for my Name to be there, nor have I chosen anyone to be the leader over my people Israel. [6] But now I have chosen Jerusalem for my Name to be there, and I have chosen David to rule my people Israel.'
>
> [7] "My father David had it in his heart to build a temple for the Name of the LORD,

the God of Israel. 8 But the LORD said to my father David, 'Because it was in your heart to build a temple for my Name, you did well to have this in your heart. 9 Nevertheless, you are not the one to build the temple, but your son, who is your own flesh and blood— he is the one who will build the temple for my Name.'

10 "The LORD has kept the promise he made. I have succeeded David my father and now I sit on the throne of Israel, just as the LORD promised, and I have built the temple for the Name of the LORD, the God of Israel. 11 There I have placed the ark, in which is the covenant of the LORD that he made with the people of Israel."   - 2 Chronicles 6:1-11

The Dedication of the Temple

1 When Solomon finished praying, fire came down from heaven and consumed the burnt offering and the sacrifices, and the glory of the LORD filled the temple. 2 The priests could not enter the temple of the LORD because the glory of the LORD filled it. 3 When all the Israelites saw the fire coming down and the glory of the LORD above the temple, they knelt on the pavement with their faces to the ground, and they worshiped and gave thanks to the LORD, saying,
"He is good; his love endures forever."

⁶ The priests took their positions, as did the Levites with the LORD's musical instruments, which King David had made for praising the LORD and which were used when he gave thanks, saying, "His love endures forever." Opposite the Levites, the priests blew their trumpets, **and all the Israelites were standing.**

- 2 Chronicles 7:1-3, 6

Again, fire came down from Heaven and consumed the offerings and sacrifices. The Glory filled the temple so much that the priests were unable to even enter let alone minister. This was also exemplified with Moses when he completed the first tabernacle (Exodus 40:34-35). And the people got it too! When the people saw this, they knelt with their faces to the ground and worshipped the Lord. When the Glory is present no one misses out. The priest' or worship leader's responsibility is to press into the Holy of Holies through worship and not give up until the Glory is present.

The Glory Returns to the Temple

¹ Then the man brought me to the gate facing east, ² and I saw the glory of the God of Israel coming from the east. His voice was

like the roar of rushing waters, and the land was radiant with his glory.

- Ezekiel 43:1-2

4 The glory of the LORD entered the temple through the gate facing east. 5 Then the Spirit lifted me up and brought me into the inner court, and the glory of the LORD filled the temple. 6 While the man was standing beside me, I heard someone speaking to me from inside the temple.

7 He said: "Son of man, this is the place of my throne and the place for the soles of my feet. This is where I will live among the Israelites forever. The house of Israel will never again defile my holy name—neither they nor their kings—by their prostitution and the lifeless idols of their kings at their high places.   - Ezekiel 43:4-7

We are beginning to see a picture of what God not only intended worship to look like but also be. As we previously explored in chapter 5, Judah, the tribe on the east side, leads off first. Judah's very name means praise and it is the tribe from of which both David and Jesus descended. And when the Glory of the Lord comes back into the Temple, it will enter through the east gate, and it is where Jesus in all of his Glory shall reappear. Yet it remains shut until he comes with his key.

¹ Then the man brought me back to the outer gate of the sanctuary, the one facing east, and it was shut. ² The LORD said to me, "This gate is to remain shut. It must not be opened; no one may enter through it. It is to remain shut because the LORD, the God of Israel, has entered through it. ³ The prince himself is the only one who may sit inside the gateway to eat in the presence of the LORD. He is to enter by way of the portico of the gateway and go out the same way."

- Ezekiel 44:1-3

I believe the east gate shall only be re-opened by the Glory of the Lord, when Jesus reenters this gate. Look at the parallel in the New Testament:

⁷ "To the angel of the church in Philadelphia write:
These are the words of him who is holy and true, who holds the key of David. What he opens no one can shut, and what he shuts no one can open.   - Revelation 3:7

Can you picture the Lord Jesus in all of his Glory with the key of David in his hands re-opening the east gate making his way back into the temple?

Preparing the Way of the Lord

I believe we are in a parallel period to that of John the Baptist who was called to prepare the way of the Lord. It is interesting that he was called to do his ministry out in the wilderness, as the Lord Jesus had not yet been given up for the salvation of man. So the people were unable to enter their spiritual "Promised Land" without the offering of the sacrificial Lamb. They were on the edge of the "Promised Land" looking in but unable to enter until Jesus was crucified and then resurrected. I believe this is why John the Baptist prepared the way of the Lord in the wilderness. However, we are called to prepare the way of the Lord in the Glory of the "Promised Land." We are to herald the coming of the King with his Glory just as they laid palm branches before him as he humbly rode in on a donkey. When he comes again it will not be on a lowly donkey but on a majestic White Horse!

Another parallel to consider: When John the Baptist first entered the scene there had been a famine of the Word of the Lord in the land for 400 years. And then Jesus, the Word made flesh, came and fed the hungry famished people the Word of God. I believe we have been in just such a famine for the Glory of the Lord.

The magnitude of which has not been experienced since the early church went into a dark age around the 4th century A.D. Fortunately for us there have been individuals whose candles have continued burning, keeping the fire from dying out throughout the centuries until now. This is why I believe strongly that the Lord will again step foot on his property and the Glory of the Lord shall come in such a way that the hungry, starved church shall be filled and satisfied with the Glory of the Lord.

Do you remember the army described in Joel 2:4-11?

> 4 **They have the appearance of horses; they gallop along like cavalry. 5 With a noise like that of chariots they leap over the mountaintops, like a crackling fire consuming stubble, like a mighty army drawn up for battle.**
>
> 6 **At the sight of them, nations are in anguish; every face turns pale.**
>
> 7 **They charge like warriors; they scale walls like soldiers. They all march in line, not swerving from their course.**
>
> 8 **They do not jostle each other; each marches straight ahead. They plunge through defenses without breaking ranks.**

⁹ They rush upon the city; they run along the wall. They climb into the houses; like thieves they enter through the windows.

¹⁰ Before them the earth shakes, the sky trembles, the sun and moon are darkened, and the stars no longer shine.

¹¹ The LORD thunders at the head of his army; his forces are beyond number, and mighty are those who obey his command. The day of the LORD is great; it is dreadful. Who can endure it?   - Joel 2:4-11

I believe God is raising up the worshipping remnant of the priesthood who will carry the Glory before the Army of the Lord described in Joel 2. They will be led of course by the Commander of Hosts, Jesus himself. Many are talking about this glorious army of Joel 2, however, who will be given charge to raise up this priesthood of Glory that shall precede the King entering his Sanctuary in Psalm 68?

²⁴ Your procession has come into view, O God, the procession of my God and King into the sanctuary.

²⁵ In front are the singers, after them the musicians; with them are the maidens playing tambourines.

²⁶ Praise God in the great congregation; praise the LORD in the assembly of Israel.
                                                    - Psalm 68:24-26

For this glorious army to rise up and fulfill its' destiny, the Lord must restore the Glory to his priesthood so that he can restore the Glory to his Church. As the priesthood, we are to go into the river and stand the ground until the entire church crosses over to where the Glory is.

The sounding of the trumpet announces the arrival of the King in all of his Glory. And he will enter again through the east gate. The Glory of the Lord shall again fill his Temple through the entrance of the King of Kings, the Prince of Peace. But his path will be prepared before him with the Glory, and we will see the Lord, high and lifted up, with Glory in the train of his robe that fills the temple. We as ministers and priests of the Lord are to precede him with his Glory that he left us, preparing the way before him.

How Close is the King's Return?

How close is the Lord from receiving his bride unto himself? Watch the bride, for she is a mirrored reflection of the Glory of the King.

She reflects his radiance as he approaches. The whole earth shall be filled with his Glory, for it shall arise within the church, his bride, heralding the coming of the King.

If the glory of the former house was so magnificent, how much more will this latter house be at the fulfillment of all things?

> [9] 'The glory of this present house will be greater than the glory of the former house,' says the LORD Almighty. 'And in this place I will grant peace,' declares the LORD Almighty."
> - Haggai 2:9

Glimpses of Heaven, Meditations of Worship

These passages are included for you to meditate upon, to visit the sights, the sounds, and the experiences of Heaven. Some are included that you may see Jesus in his glorious image. Use the key of the imagination (spiritual meditation upon these passages as pertaining to worship) to unlock the spiritual and prophetic doors that can bring these passages alive for you. They were chosen to evoke the spirit of worship. Visit as often as you can.

A Picture of Jesus

[12] I turned around to see the voice that was speaking to me. And when I turned I saw seven golden lamp stands, [13] and among the lamp stands was someone "like a son of man," dressed in a robe reaching down to his feet and with a golden sash around his chest. [14] His head and hair were white like wool, as white as snow, and his eyes were like blazing fire. [15] His feet were like bronze

glowing in a furnace, and his voice was like the sound of rushing waters. ¹⁶ In his right hand he held seven stars, and out of his mouth came a sharp double-edged sword. His face was like the sun shining in all its brilliance.

¹⁷ When I saw him, I fell at his feet as though dead. Then he placed his right hand on me and said: "Do not be afraid. I am the First and the Last. ¹⁸ I am the Living One; I was dead, and behold I am alive for ever and ever! And I hold the keys of death and Hades. - Revelation 1:12-18

²⁵ Then there came a voice from above the expanse over their heads as they stood with lowered wings. ²⁶ Above the expanse over their heads was what looked like a throne of sapphire, and high above on the throne was a figure like that of a man. ²⁷ I saw that from what appeared to be his waist up he looked like glowing metal, as if full of fire, and that from there down he looked like fire; and brilliant light surrounded him. ²⁸ Like the appearance of a rainbow in the clouds on a rainy day, so was the radiance around him. This was the appearance of the likeness of the glory of the LORD. When I saw it, I fell facedown, and I heard the voice of one speaking. - Ezekiel 1:25-28

¹ In the sixth year, in the sixth month on the fifth day, while I was sitting in my house and the elders of Judah were sitting before me, the hand of the Sovereign LORD came upon me there. ² I looked, and I saw a figure like that of a man. From what appeared to be his waist down he was like fire, and from there up his appearance was as bright as glowing metal.

³ He stretched out what looked like a hand and took me by the hair of my head. The Spirit lifted me up between earth and heaven and in visions of God he took me to Jerusalem, to the entrance to the north gate of the inner court, where the idol that provokes to jealousy stood. ⁴ And there before me was the glory of the God of Israel, as in the vision I had seen in the plain.

- Ezekiel 8: 1-4

The Throne in Heaven

¹ After this I looked, and there before me was a door standing open in heaven. And the voice I had first heard speaking to me like a trumpet said, "Come up here, and I will show you what must take place after this." ² At once I was in the Spirit, and there before me was a throne in heaven with someone sitting on it. ³ And the one who sat there had the appearance of jasper and car-

nelian. A rainbow, resembling an emerald, encircled the throne. 4 Surrounding the throne were twenty-four other thrones, and seated on them were twenty-four elders. They were dressed in white and had crowns of gold on their heads.

5 From the throne came flashes of lightning, rumblings and peals of thunder. Before the throne, seven lamps were blazing. These are the seven spirits of God. 6 Also before the throne there was what looked like a sea of glass, clear as crystal. In the center, around the throne, were four living creatures, and they were covered with eyes, in front and in back. 7 The first living creature was like a lion, the second was like an ox, the third had a face like a man, the fourth was like a flying eagle.

8 Each of the four living creatures had six wings and was covered with eyes all around, even under his wings. Day and night they never stop saying: "Holy, holy, holy is the Lord God Almighty, who was, and is, and is to come." 9 Whenever the living creatures give glory, honor and thanks to him who sits on the throne and who lives for ever and ever,

10 the twenty-four elders fall down before him who sits on the throne, and worship him who lives for ever and ever. They lay their crowns before the throne and say:

11"You are worthy, our Lord and God, to receive glory and honor and power, for you created all things, and by your will they were created and have their being."

- Revelation 4

The Scroll and the Lamb

1 Then I saw in the right hand of him who sat on the throne a scroll with writing on both sides and sealed with seven seals. 2 And I saw a mighty angel proclaiming in a loud voice, "Who is worthy to break the seals and open the scroll?" 3 But no one in heaven or on earth or under the earth could open the scroll or even look inside it. 4 I wept and wept because no one was found who was worthy to open the scroll or look inside. 5 Then one of the elders said to me, "Do not weep! See, the Lion of the tribe of Judah, the Root of David, has triumphed. He is able to open the scroll and its seven seals."

6 Then I saw a Lamb, looking as if it had been slain, standing in the center of the throne, encircled by the four living creatures and the elders. He had seven horns and seven eyes, which are the seven spirits of God sent out into all the earth. 7 He came and took the scroll from the right hand of him who sat on the throne.

⁸ And when he had taken it, the four living creatures and the twenty-four elders fell down before the Lamb. Each one had a harp and they were holding golden bowls full of incense, which are the prayers of the saints.
⁹ And they sang a new song:
"You are worthy to take the scroll
and to open its seals,
because you were slain,
and with your blood you purchased men for God
from every tribe and language and people and nation.

¹⁰ You have made them to be a kingdom and priests to serve our God, and they will reign on the earth."

¹¹ Then I looked and heard the voice of many angels, numbering thousands upon thousands, and ten thousand times ten thousand. They encircled the throne and the living creatures and the elders.

¹² In a loud voice they sang:
"Worthy is the Lamb, who was slain,
to receive power and wealth and wisdom and strength
and honor and glory and praise!"

¹³ Then I heard every creature in heaven and on earth and under the earth and on the sea, and all that is in them, singing:
"To him who sits on the throne and to the Lamb

be praise and honor and glory and power, for ever and ever!"

14 The four living creatures said, "Amen," and the elders fell down and worshiped.
- Revelation 5:1-14

Hallelujah!

1After this I heard what sounded like the roar of a great multitude in heaven shouting:
"Hallelujah!
Salvation and glory and power belong to our God,
2for true and just are his judgments.
He has condemned the great prostitute
who corrupted the earth by her adulteries.
He has avenged on her the blood of his servants."

3And again they shouted:
"Hallelujah!
The smoke from her goes up for ever and ever."

4The twenty-four elders and the four living creatures fell down and worshiped God, who was seated on the throne. And they cried:
"Amen, Hallelujah!"

5Then a voice came from the throne, saying:
"Praise our God,
all you his servants,

you who fear him,
both small and great!"

⁶Then I heard what sounded like a great
multitude, like the roar of rushing waters
and like loud peals of thunder, shouting:
"Hallelujah!
For our Lord God Almighty reigns.
⁷Let us rejoice and be glad
and give him glory!
For the wedding of the Lamb has come,
and his bride has made herself ready.

⁸Fine linen, bright and clean,
was given her to wear." (Fine linen stands
for the righteous acts of the saints.)

⁹Then the angel said to me, "Write: 'Blessed
are those who are invited to the wedding
supper of the Lamb!' " And he added, "These
are the true words of God."

¹⁰At this I fell at his feet to worship him.
But he said to me, "Do not do it! I am a fellow servant with you and with your brothers
who hold to the testimony of Jesus. Worship
God! <u>For the testimony of Jesus is the spirit
of prophecy</u>."   - Revelation 19:1-10

The Rider on the White Horse

¹¹ I saw heaven standing open and there before me was a white horse, whose rider is
called Faithful and True. With justice he

220

judges and makes war. [12] His eyes are like blazing fire, and on his head are many crowns. He has a name written on him that no one knows but he himself. [13] He is dressed in a robe dipped in blood, and his name is the Word of God.

[14] The armies of heaven were following him, riding on white horses and dressed in fine linen, white and clean. [15] Out of his mouth comes a sharp sword with which to strike down the nations. "He will rule them with an iron scepter." He treads the winepress of the fury of the wrath of God Almighty. [16] On his robe and on his thigh he has this name written:
KING OF KINGS AND LORD OF LORDS.

- Revelation 19:11-16

The New Jerusalem

[1] Then I saw a new heaven and a new earth, for the first heaven and the first earth had passed away, and there was no longer any sea. [2] I saw the Holy City, the new Jerusalem, coming down out of heaven from God, prepared as a bride beautifully dressed for her husband. [3] And I heard a loud voice from the throne saying, "Now the dwelling of God is with men, and he will live with them. They will be his people, and God himself will be with them and be their God.

⁴ He will wipe every tear from their eyes. There will be no more death or mourning or crying or pain, for the old order of things has passed away."

⁵ He who was seated on the throne said, "I am making everything new!" Then he said, "Write this down, for these words are trustworthy and true."

⁶ He said to me: "It is done. I am the Alpha and the Omega, the Beginning and the End. To him who is thirsty I will give to drink without cost from the spring of the water of life. ⁷ He who overcomes will inherit all this, and I will be his God and he will be my son. ⁸ But the cowardly, the unbelieving, the vile, the murderers, the sexually immoral, those who practice magic arts, the idolaters and all liars—their place will be in the fiery lake of burning sulfur. This is the second death."

⁹ One of the seven angels who had the seven bowls full of the seven last plagues came and said to me, "Come, I will show you the bride, the wife of the Lamb." ¹⁰ And he carried me away in the Spirit to a mountain great and high, and showed me the Holy City, Jerusalem, coming down out of heaven from God. ¹¹ It shone with the glory of God, and its brilliance was like that of a very precious jewel, like a jasper, clear as crystal. ¹² It had a great, high wall with twelve gates,

and with twelve angels at the gates. On the gates were written the names of the twelve tribes of Israel. [13] There were three gates on the east, three on the north, three on the south and three on the west. [14] The wall of the city had twelve foundations, and on them were the names of the twelve apostles of the Lamb.

[15] The angel who talked with me had a measuring rod of gold to measure the city, its gates and its walls. [16] The city was laid out like a square, as long as it was wide. He measured the city with the rod and found it to be 12,000 stadia in length, and as wide and high as it is long.

[17] He measured its wall and it was 144 cubits thick, by man's measurement, which the angel was using. [18] The wall was made of jasper, and the city of pure gold, as pure as glass. [19] The foundations of the city walls were decorated with every kind of precious stone. The first foundation was jasper, the second sapphire, the third chalcedony, the fourth emerald, [20] the fifth sardonyx, the sixth carnelian, the seventh chrysolite, the eighth beryl, the ninth topaz, the tenth chrysoprase, the eleventh jacinth, and the twelfth amethyst. [21] The twelve gates were twelve pearls, each gate made of a single pearl. The great street of the city was of pure gold, like transparent glass.

²² I did not see a temple in the city, because the Lord God Almighty and the Lamb are its temple. ²³ The city does not need the sun or the moon to shine on it, for the glory of God gives it light, and the Lamb is its lamp. ²⁴ The nations will walk by its light, and the kings of the earth will bring their splendor into it. ²⁵ On no day will its gates ever be shut, for there will be no night there. ²⁶ The glory and honor of the nations will be brought into it. ²⁷ Nothing impure will ever enter it, nor will anyone who does what is shameful or deceitful, but only those whose names are written in the Lamb's book of life.   - Revelation 21:1-27

Source Notes

1. On page 61, 117 and 130, reference is made to Ray Hughes and his CD series, *The Minstrel Series.*

2. All scripture quotations, unless otherwise indicated, are taken from the HOLY BIBLE, NEW INTERNATIONAL VERSION®. NIV®. Copyright © 1973, 1978, 1984 by International Bible Society. Used by permission of Zondervan. All rights reserved. "The "NIV" and "New International Version" trademarks are registered in the United States Patent and Trademark Office by International Bible Society."

3. Scripture quotations marked (AMP) are taken from the Amplified Bible, Copyright © 1954, 1958, 1962, 1964, 1965, 1987 by The Lockman Foundation. Used by permission.

4. Scriptures marked KJV are from the KING JAMES VERSION.

Source Notes

1. On page 61, reference is made to Ray Hughes and his CD series, *The Minstrel Series.*

2. On page 117, reference is made to Ray Hughes and his CD series, *The Minstrel Series.*

3. All scriptural references are NIV (New International Version), unless stated specifically as KJV (King James Version) or AMP (Amplified).